# CONTENTS

CW01481140

# SUMMARY

The premise of most Western thinking on counter-insurgency is that success depends on establishing a perception of legitimacy among local populations. The path to legitimacy is often seen as the improvement of governance in the form of effective and efficient administration of government and public services. However, good governance is not the only possible basis for claims to legitimacy. This monograph considers whether, in insurgencies where ethno-religious identities are politically salient, claims to legitimacy may rest more on the identity of who governs, rather than on how those people govern. Building on a synthesis of scholarship and policy regarding insurgencies and counterinsurgencies, the politics of ethnic identity, governance, and legitimacy, the author presents an analytic framework for examining these issues and then applies that framework to two detailed local case studies of American counterinsurgency operations in Iraq: Ramadi from 2004-05; and Tal Afar from 2005-06. These case studies are based on primary research, including dozens of interviews with participants and eyewitnesses.

In Ramadi, identity politics clearly trumped quality of governance in shaping the course of events. The grievances that fueled the insurgency had far more to do with a deep sense of disenfranchisement within Iraq's Sunni community and the related fear of sectarian persecution than it did with any failure in the government's performance. As a result, the evidence from this case points toward major limits to how much popular loyalty and legitimacy could be won through the improvement of governance. Other factors—namely security itself and identity-based concepts of legitimate rule (both tribal and sectarian) — appeared more decisive during the time of the case study. Moreover, the tribal "Awakening" movement that took hold in Ramadi the following year strongly supports this interpretation of events. The Awakening seems to have stemmed from two key changes in Ramadi and its surrounding Anbar province. First was the exhaustion of the population with violence and terror at the hands of Islamic extremists in their midst. Second was a new willingness of the Coalition to recognize the legitimacy of local tribal rule in spite of the sectarian tension this rule introduced between local and national sovereignty.

Tal Afar's story is quite different, but suggests a similar conclusion. While the quality of governance mattered in the way both the population and the counterinsurgents perceived legitimacy, improvements in governance in Tal Afar were more a consequence than a cause of successful counterinsurgency. Without both the U.S. Army's dense presence in the city and its intensive focus on brokering compromises among the city's largely sectarian tribal conflicts, improvements in governance likely would never have taken root. Governance and political compromise between sectarian groups clearly reinforced each other there, but interviews with participants in the counterinsurgency in Tal Afar suggest that improvements in governance were of secondary importance in reducing violence in the city.

The cases examined here yield ample evidence that ethno-religious identity politics do shape counterinsurgency outcomes in important ways, and also offer qualified support for the argument that addressing identity politics may be more critical than good governance to counterinsurgent success. However, the cases do not discredit the utility to counterinsurgents of providing good governance, and they corroborate the traditional view that population security is the most important element of successful counterinsurgency strategy. Key policy implications include the importance of making strategy development as sensitive as possible to the dynamics of identity politics, and to local variations and the complexity in causal relationships among popular loyalties, grievances, and political violence.

*If you're not confused, then you don't know how complex the situation is.*

Lieutenant General Jim Mattis
United States Marine Corps,
Anbar Province, April 2004[1]

*It is so damn complex. If you ever think you have the solution to this, you're wrong, and you're dangerous.*

Colonel H. R. McMaster
U.S. Army,
Tal Afar, February 2006[2]

---

1. Thomas E. Ricks, *Fiasco: The American Military Adventure in Iraq*, New York: Penguin Press, 2006, p. 343.

2. George Packer, "Letter from Iraq: The Lessons of Tal Afar," *The New Yorker*, April 10, 2006, p. 57.

# CHAPTER 1

## ANALYZING GOVERNANCE AND IDENTITY POLITICS IN COUNTERINSURGENCY

### INTRODUCTION

This monograph[1] was born of an attempt to make sense of two strong but somewhat contradictory intuitions about counterinsurgency. The first intuition is captured by an Iraqi Sunni tribal leader's comment that Iraq's Shi'a Muslims "cannot take charge of Iraq in the same manner as the Sunnis. The [Shi'a] are backwards. They are barbarian savages. . . ."[2] From this perspective, in civil conflict it matters who is in charge, and the ability of any party to succeed—insurgent or counterinsurgent—is at least partly a function of who they are, not just how they behave. Clearly, conflict is often rooted deeply in the politics of group identities and in such cases, the principal objective of the insurgents may be to overturn rule by some "other" group. In such a case, settling the conflict over identity politics would become one of the keys to resolving the broader conflict.

But the second intuition is that what most people want overwhelmingly is just a peaceful life where they can work, raise their children, provide for their families and have a society that functions and provides them the security and essential services that they need. Again, an example from Iraq illustrates the point. A woman in Baghdad told a reporter, "We want security and we want stability. Anyone who comes along is fine as long as he brings security and stability."[3] Or as an American Soldier put it, "He who is able to fix the public utilities holds the keys to the kingdom in

1

terms of winning the support of the Iraqi people and ultimately ending this conflict."[4] By this way of thinking, resolving the conflict in insurgencies is all about establishing good governance. If the counterinsurgent can manage to give people a good life, they will have a stake in the status quo and will abandon their support for the insurgents who threaten that status quo.

Each of these two intuitions implies a priority for counterinsurgency strategy. If people fight over ethnic or religious identity, then counterinsurgents must get the incumbent political system to deal effectively with the distribution of power across those groups. If people fight over provision of basic governance, then counterinsurgents must ensure that they are capable of "outgoverning" their insurgent opponents. While both of these intuitions can be valid to some degree, they are also not entirely compatible with each other. If different groups of people under a common system really oppose each other for who they are, or conceive of their political interests within ethnically-defined boundaries, then how much should a counterinsurgent expect to achieve by making the electricity and the sewers work, and by providing employment? Conversely, if all people want is a peaceful, comfortable life, why have ethnic and religious group loyalties seemed so often to have subverted counterinsurgents' attempts to improve governance in conflict-stricken lands?

The recent wars in Iraq and Afghanistan have made the tension between these intuitions increasingly evident in American counterinsurgency policy and military doctrine. The counterinsurgency field manual published by the U.S. Army and Marine Corps in December 2006 states that "The primary objective of any counterinsurgent is to foster the development of effective governance by a legitimate government."[5] This judgment is in keeping with a conventional wisdom about counterinsurgency strategy that has accumulated over several decades of war and scholarship. Its premise, like that of most Western thinking on counterinsurgency, is that success depends on establishing a perception of legitimacy for the ruling regime in some critical portion of the local population. Among the mechanisms available to counterinsurgents for establishing that legitimacy, the most prominent in both practice and doctrine has been the improvement of governance in the form of effective and efficient administration of government and public services. Good governance, by this logic, is the key to "winning hearts and minds."[6]

Beginning in 2003, the U.S. struggle to manage expanding sectarian civil conflict in Iraq began to call this traditional logic into question. As Central Intelligence Agency (CIA) Director Michael Hayden told the Iraq Study Group in December 2006:

> The current situation, with regard to governance in Iraq, was probably irreversible in the short term, because of the world views of many of the [Iraqi] government leaders, which were shaped by a sectarian filter and a government that was organized for its ethnic and religious balance rather than competence or capacity. . . . The Iraqi identity is muted. The Sunni or Shi'a identity is foremost.[7]

What the Iraqi experience was suggesting was that good governance is not the only plausible basis for claims to legitimacy among contending political factions, especially in environments where ethnic or religious identities are politically salient. Instead, perhaps in such conflicts, claims to legitimacy may rest

3

primarily on the identity of *who* governs, rather than on *how* they govern.

In this light, is good governance even necessary to defeat insurgencies in cases like Iraq? Or, to formulate the question more precisely: *In the presence of major ethno-religious cleavages, does good governance contribute much less to counterinsurgent success than efforts toward reaching political agreements that directly address those cleavages?*

This is the question this monograph will address. Its focus in marshalling evidence to help answer the question is on two detailed local cases of American counterinsurgency operations in Iraq: in Ramadi from 2004-05; and in Tal Afar from 2005-06. This introductory chapter provides some context for analysis in three dimensions:

- A summary of scholarship and policy regarding governance, identity politics and counterinsurgency;
- An analytic framework for organizing case study evidence, and a discussion of methodological challenges inherent in the subject;
- An explanation for the choice of case studies.

## Conceptual and Historical Perspectives on Governance, Identity, Politics, and Counterinsurgency.

Understanding the roots of modern counterinsurgency strategy as practiced by the United States and its allies requires careful synthesis of ideas and empirical insights from a wide range of academic disciplines and historical experiences that bear on the complex interactions among concepts of legitimacy, governance, and political violence. The central question posed by this analysis demands the addition of theories and history related to ethno-religious identity and conflict to the list.

An earlier article attempted to provide just such a synthesis of prior analysis and experience, and so this monograph will not devote much space to a detailed examination of these conceptual foundations.[8] That article established a few important premises, which can be summarized as follows.

Recent policy and strategy for counterinsurgency in the United States strongly reflect conventional wisdom forged in the 1950s and 1960s in response to formative experiences in that era, the heyday of Maoist people's wars, modernization theory, and Cold War great power competition. In particular, conception of counterinsurgency as a competition of governance between insurgents and counterinsurgents is based on materialistic views of social welfare, justice, and legitimate authority from that era that are not universally held. The resulting prescription for counterinsurgents of winning hearts and minds, while rhetorically flexible enough to transcend narrow interpretation, is, historically speaking, firmly rooted in the mid-20th century intellectual tradition of the Cold War and decolonization.

It is also important to note that both the competing liberal and the communist sides of this intellectual tradition are relatively insensitive to the divisive potential of ethnic and religious identity politics in civil conflicts. This is true partly for diametrically opposed reasons: a normative emphasis on political pluralism in the liberal case, and a dedication to a singular cosmopolitan set of values in the communist case. But it is also partly true for a common reason: the materialist conception of legitimacy noted above, which

5

leaves little room for consideration of differing ethno-religious claims to legitimate political authority.

Nevertheless, despite the marginal role that identity politics have played in shaping ideas about counterinsurgency, a substantial body of scholarship from the past few decades establishes that conflicts where ethnic and religious identities are politically salient have different dynamics than other conflicts. Experiences in Iraq and Afghanistan have prompted a fresh appreciation for the importance of this factor in counterinsurgency, thus making it ripe for systematic evaluation, especially given the new wealth of empirical evidence emerging from recent battlefields.

**Methodological Considerations and an Analytic Framework.**

Counterinsurgency and the politics of ethnic identity clearly pose formidable analytical challenges. Relevant variables are legion, their interactions are complex, their descriptions subjective, and their associated data messy. As with other complex phenomena, great simplifications are sometimes necessary to make a given problem analytically tractable. The trick is to create a depiction of the world that is simple enough to make data available, questions coherent, and answers comprehensible, but no simpler than that.

The first step in this direction is to examine the basic causal logic usually hypothesized between counterinsurgency strategies and the ultimate defeat of insurgents. In the most general sense, counterinsurgency strategy can be divided into two classes of activities: improving governance and providing security. The U.S. Government's *Counterinsurgency Guide* frames the problem of counterinsurgency strategy this way: "Effective COIN [counterinsurgency] . . . in-volves a careful balance between constructive dimensions (building effective and legitimate government) and destructive dimensions (destroying the insurgent movements)."[9] As political scientist D. Michael Shafer describes this logic, "[American counterinsurgency] doctrine emphasizes development *and* security. . . . Without security, so the argument goes, development is impossible; without good government and economic progress, efforts to maintain it will be bootless."[10]

Figure 1-1 outlines this logic, with events labeled A-H and causal processes labeled 1-9. In event A, counterinsurgents attempt to improve governance through the variety of mechanisms discussed in the definition above. At the same time, they also conduct traditional security operations, including both police and military operations (event C). If improvements in governance occur (event B via processes 1 and 2), then this should win popular loyalty and support for the government and thereby decrease popular support for the insurgency (event D). This should then cause the insurgency to decline (event G) both directly, as it is denied safe havens and recruits (process 5), and indirectly, as the population grows more cooperative with counterinsurgent security operations (events E and F and processes 6-8). Finally, the declining insurgency eventually results in a stable peace (process 9 and event H). This, in essence, is the conventional explanation offered by much of the academic literature and operational doctrine on counterinsurgency for an observed correlation between events A (attempts to improve governance) and H (a resulting stable peace).

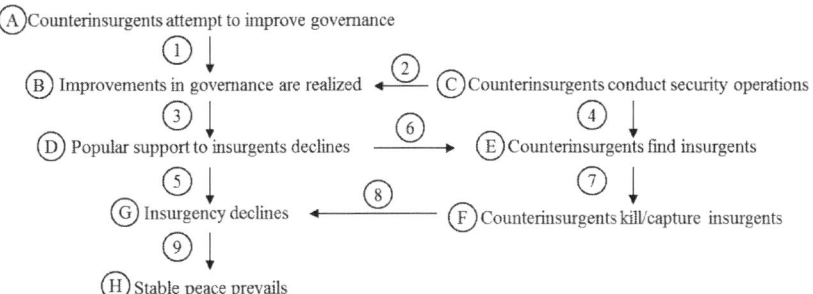

**Figure 1-1. Basic Causal Logic of Counterinsurgency Strategy.**

If, however, we observe A but do not observe any evidence of H over time, we can infer that one or more of the causal processes in this chain has not operated as hypothesized. Specifically, what might those breakdowns be? Possibilities could be found in any one of the processes depicted in Figure 1-1, but this study focuses particular attention on process number 3: the mechanism that translates improved governance into shifting loyalties among the affected population. For it is here that legitimacy is widely believed to reside and to operate as a key instrument of the counterinsurgent. It is here that conflicts involving identity may subvert the intended effects of improvements in governance on popular support for the insurgency.

One of the principal problems with legitimacy as an analytic construct, of course, is that it is an abstraction, and therefore very difficult to observe. A little like dark matter in astrophysics, it is recognizable primarily through its imputed effects. In the model depicted here, these effects would be visible in events E, G, and ultimately H. But this indirect inference of the causal role of legitimacy is problematic because each of these signal events (E, G, and H) can also be caused by events C, E, and F. Moreover, events C, E, and F can plausibly operate without significant contribution from the chain of legitimacy building, events A, B, and D. For this reason, we cannot necessarily infer a causal relationship between events A and H, even when they correlate.

In fact, the conceptual challenge here is even thornier than this problem with legitimacy implies. An additional complication arises from the fact that security is both an important input and an important output of any counterinsurgency strategy. This has two troublesome logical implications.

First, "Stable peace" (event H) may sometimes be difficult to distinguish from the security operations depicted here as event C. Sharp reductions in the magnitude and frequency of insurgent violence represent probably the clearest available indicator of the overall success of a counterinsurgent effort. But such reductions can often be provided fairly readily, if only temporarily, with sufficient quantities of patrols by police or military forces. This kind of militarized security could hardly be described as a successful counterinsurgency, however. The real measure of success would have to be the relative absence of violence coupled with much smaller levels of force. Political scientist Jeffrey Race refers to these two different types of security as tactical and strategic security, respectively.[11] Distinguishing between the two empirically is certainly feasible, but it requires both explicit collection and interpretation of the data in these terms, and a considerable degree of subjectivity in the interpretation of the events.

The second logical implication, following from the first, concerns process number 2 in Figure 1-1. This reflects the fact that improvements in security are likely to help allow improvements in governance in addition to, or instead of, the other way around. If an observed improvement in security could, in fact, be either event C or event H, then we cannot be sure whether event B is actually a cause of improved security or an effect. This potential for confusion about cause and effect is not simply a methodological problem. It is an operational problem that strikes at the heart of strategy and decisionmaking. As one reporter described this problem in relating the struggles of an American provincial reconstruction team in Baqubah, ". . . officials seemed unable to agree on whether poor security was preventing reconstruction or whether reconstruction failures had caused security to erode."[12] In such an environment, what is the strategist or the analyst to do?

The key to better understanding of complex phenomena such as these is in examining the detailed course of events in which the relevant variables interacted. A focus on this level of detail offers the only hope of being able to reliably navigate the ambiguities outlined above. An empirical focus on the national level, on simply establishing correlations among variables, or on achieving a large sample size for statistical analysis could not accommodate the interpretive burden demanded by the dynamics under examination.[13]

Moreover, measurement of abstract phenomena such as governance, identity, and counterinsurgent success is inherently difficult. While no methodological panacea for this challenge exists, it is possible to achieve some degree of reliability in such measurement through the collection of perspectives from direct observers of and participants in the events. This kind of first-hand data is available in a few different forms: government and military archival resources such as after-action reports, lessons learned, and unit histories; extensive reporting by journalists of a diverse range of nationalities and perspectives; and interviews with military and civilian personnel who have worked in Iraq. This study draws on all three of these forms.

With all of these considerations in mind, the case studies presented are organized around a simple analytic framework consisting of five questions:

1. Were ethno-religious identity-based cleavages significant?

2. Was good governance provided?

3. Were political agreements addressing ethno-religious cleavages pursued?

4. Were good security operations conducted?

5. Was the counterinsurgency successful?

Specifically, what does each of these terms mean, and what information is required to answer the questions?

*Ethno-religious Identity-Based Cleavages:* Identities of interest here are those that are group-based, related to ethnic or religious affiliations, and manifest in political behavior. Hence, the term "ethno-religious" describes group identity and behavior associated with either ethnicity, religion, or both together.

Ethno-religious identities are present everywhere, but they are not equally politically salient everywhere. The term "cleavage" describes the presence of multiple politically salient ethno-religious identities within a single political unit. The term is rooted in theories of political sociology that distinguish societies with dominant "segmental cleavages" from those with dominant "cross-cutting cleavages."[14] With segmental cleavages, individuals' interests across multiple domains such as ethnicity, religion, class, profession,

11

region, etc., tend to align in discrete social segments. With cross-cutting cleavages, interests which cross multiple domains do not align particularly well, thus preventing strong linkages between group identity and political cohesiveness. The ethno-religious identity-based cleavages of interest here are segmental cleavages, and thus of high political salience.

*Good Governance:* "Good governance" is effective and efficient administration of public services and allocation of public resources. As such, assessment of the quality of governance will focus on issues such as economic organization, public health, education, the justice system, sanitation, power, and water. The definition used here is broader than some definitions of governance, notably the one offered by the U.S. military's latest manual on counterinsurgency. There, governance is defined as one of six separate "lines of operation," which "relates to the host nation's ability to gather and distribute resources while providing direction and control for society." While the activities that the counterinsurgency manual identifies with governance are included in the definition used here, so are activities that the manual identifies with two other lines of operation: "essential services," dealing with the operation of power, water, sanitation, education, medical systems and the like; and "economic development," dealing with the supervision and regulation of a functioning economy that provides employment and creates and allocates resources.[15]

*Political Agreements Directly Addressing Cleavages:* Such agreements may take many different forms. These might include the establishment of consociational power-sharing mechanisms, arrangements of ethno-religious group autonomy, or perhaps electoral arrangements designed to foster greater cross-group cooperation. The key qualifying criterion is that the political agreement expressly recognizes the extant cleavage in trying to resolve conflict.

*Good Security Operations and Success:* As described above, distinguishing security operations as an input to counterinsurgency from the enduring condition of security that results from successful counterinsurgency is a delicate but crucial part of any strategic analysis of this topic. In looking for metrics that might define success, security is the most obvious candidate. Event H in Figure 1-1, "Stable peace prevails," represents the essence of this metric. But to reiterate the earlier point, security is both an input and an output of counterinsurgency operations. Hence, simply using security to define success introduces a serious so-called "endogeneity" problem into the research design. The hazard here is the potential for mistaking the direction of causation between the effectiveness of governance-related activities and the intensity of the insurgency. If success in the counterinsurgency is defined only according to the prevailing level of security, and some threshold level of security is necessary to execute governance-type measures, then there is some level of violence at which it is impossible to test any hypotheses about the effects of governance on levels of violence.

One possible response to this is to analyze only cases where the level of violence remains below this notional threshold. But this is impractical for the Iraq cases and would also have the drawback of excluding a significant portion of the problem from consideration. Another response would be to treat security as a trailing indicator, i.e., by comparing governance-related initiatives in month X to security in month X+1 or X+2. This avoids confusion regarding the direction of causation and also probably better represents the nature of any expected effects.[16]

Ultimately, distinguishing between the short-term security provided directly by military and police operations from more sustainable, stable security requires either retrospect through significant passage of time, or the judgment of people intimately familiar with the evolving situation. For the case studies, this monograph will emphasize the latter, identifying success and failure in instances where explicit or imputed counterinsurgent objectives, commensurate with the geographic and temporal scope under consideration, are either demonstrable and/or judged to be met by key parties to the conflict.

In summary, the methodological challenges presented by this research are formidable. Even the most careful research design will yield conclusions that are tentative and suggestive rather than decisive. Nevertheless, the importance of the subject matter compels the work. It is worth emphasizing that the methodological challenges facing questions such as those posed here have parallels in the operational world. For example, the complexities of constructing a reliable measure for success in counterinsurgency are more than academic. The counterinsurgent must wrestle with similar questions about defining success in order to build a rational, coherent strategy.[17]

## Case Study Selection.

A common theme of first-hand accounts of counterinsurgency in Iraq has been the primacy of local conditions in explaining the course of events. Coalition Provisional Authority official Rory Stewart found that:

> . . . [W]hat mattered most were local details, daily encounters with men of which we knew little and of

whom Iraqis knew little more. . . . We prefer the universal and the theoretical: the historical analogy and the statistics. But politics is local, the catastrophe of Iraq is discovered best through individual interactions.[18]

As outlined above, the need to examine the issues in a fair amount of detail also drives the focus of this paper to local level case studies. The two cases considered are the experiences of the U.S. Army's 2nd Brigade Combat Team, 2nd Infantry Division, in and around Ramadi, from September 2004 to July 2005, and the experiences of the U.S. Army's 3rd Armored Cavalry Regiment, in and around Tal Afar, from April 2005 to February 2006.

Of all the potential case studies to choose from, why do these two rise to the top? Together, six factors constitute the rationale for these selections.

1. The choice to examine two cases rather than three or 10 is driven by time constraints. More cases are always desirable, but trading depth for breadth would defeat the purpose of this analysis, so two comparative cases will suffice to shed light on the monograph's main question.

2. A superficial examination of these two cases suggests that they share a positive value on the framework's key conditional variable—the significance of ethno-religious cleavages—while having differing values for the outcome of counterinsurgent success. This combination is analytically desirable in seeking to explain which of the other variables (security, governance, or political agreements) may help to explain the differing outcomes.[19]

3. There is value in comparing cases from similar time frames.

4. There is value in comparing cases with similar insurgent threats.

5. The time frame covered by these cases — late 2004 to early 2006 — has some analytically useful properties. The Iraqi government became sovereign in June 2004, so this period avoids crossing over the transition of control between Coalition and Iraqi authority. At the same time, this period precedes a couple of key environmental shifts: the February 2006 Samarra mosque bombing and the 2007 "surge" of increased U.S. forces and changed tactics. During this time, the insurgency in the western and northern parts of Iraq was somewhat mature. Most of the large set-piece battles, such as those in Najaf, Sadr City, and the first assault on Fallujah were past, and U.S. operations had settled into a focus on counterinsurgency.

6. Ramadi has an additional attractive property, which is that it underwent a famous reversal of fortunes in late 2006 and 2007 in the form of the so-called Tribal Awakening. This research will not include a separate case study on this development, but a simple comparison between the 2004-05 case and the subsequent dramatic turn-around is relevant to the questions examined by this analysis.

## ENDNOTES - CHAPTER 1

1. This monograph was adapted from a doctoral dissertation by Michael F. Fitzsimmons, *Governance, Identity, and Counterinsurgency Strategy*, unpublished dissertation, University of Maryland, 2009. Portions of that dissertation, including a few paragraphs included in this monograph were published previously in Michael Fitzsimmons, "Hard Hearts and Open Minds? Governance, Identity, and the Intellectual Foundations of Counterinsurgency Strategy," *Journal of Strategic Studies*, Vol. 31, No. 3, June 2008.

2. Ahmed Hashim, *Insurgency and Counterinsurgency in Iraq*, Ithaca, NY: Cornell University Press, 2006, pp. 71-72.

3. Anthony Shadid, *Night Draws Near: Iraq's People in the Shadow of America's War*, New York: Henry Holt and Company, 2005, p. 149.

4. Michael R. Gordon, "In Baghdad, Struggle Ties Security to Basic Services," *New York Times*, April 22, 2008, p. 1.

5. *Field Manual (FM) 3-24/Marine Corps Warfighting Publication 3-33.5, Counterinsurgency,* Washington, DC: Headquarters, Department of the Army; Headquarters, Marine Corps Combat Development Command, Department of the Navy, December 2006, p. 1-21. Hereafter, this document will be referred to as FM 3-24/MCWP 3-33.5.

6. The first use of the phrase "hearts and minds" in the context of revolutionary warfare is often attributed to the British administrator during part of the 1948–60 Malayan Emergency, Lieutenant-General (later Field Marshal) Sir Gerald Templer, who argued in 1952 that "the answer lies not in pouring more troops into the jungle, but in the hearts and minds of the people." See Richard L. Clutterbuck, *The Long, Long War; Counterinsurgency in Malaya and Vietnam*, New York: Praeger 1966, p. 3; and Richard Stubbs, *Hearts and Minds in Guerrilla Warfare: The Malayan Emergency 1948-1960*, Oxford, UK: OUP, 1989, pp. 1–2.

7. Quoted in Bob Woodward, "CIA Said Instability Seemed 'Irreversible,'" *Washington Post*, July 12, 2007, p. 1.

8. See Fitzsimmons, "Hard Hearts and Open Minds?"

9. *U.S. Government Counterinsurgency Guide,* Washington, DC: U.S. Government Interagency Counterinsurgency Initiative, January 2009, p. 14.

10. D. Michael Shafer, *Deadly Paradigms: The Failure of U.S. Counterinsurgency Policy,* Princeton, NJ: Princeton University Press, 1988, p. 79 (emphasis in original). Other analyses employing two similar categories to describe counterinsurgency strategy include Jim Baker, "Systems Thinking and Counterinsurgencies,"

*Parameters*, Vol. 36, No. 4, Winter 2006-07, pp. 26-43; Alice Hills, "Hearts and Minds or Search and Destroy? Controlling Civilians in Urban Operations," *Small Wars and Insurgencies*, Vol. 13, No. 2, Spring 2002, p. 6; and William J. Hurley, Joel Resnick, and Alec Wahlman, *Improving Capabilities for Irregular Warfare, Vol. I: Main Text,* Alexandria, VA: Institute for Defense Analyses, 2007, p. II-3, and Appendix A.

11. Jeffrey Race, *War Comes to Long An: Revolutionary Conflict in a Vietnamese Province*, Berkeley, CA: University of California Press, 1972, p. 146.

12. Solomon Moore, "A Promising Iraqi Province is Now a Tinderbox," *Los Angeles Times*, January 3, 2007, p. 1.

13. This methodological judgment is one basis for the growing body of literature on "microlevel research" on social phenomena. For example, see Stathis N. Kalyvas, *The Logic of Violence in Civil War,* Cambridge, UK: Cambridge University Press, 2006.

14. See Seymour M. Lipset, *Political Man,* Garden City, NY: Anchor Books, 1963; Arendt Lijphart, *Democracy in Plural Societies: A Comparative Exploration,* New Haven, CT: Yale University Press, 1977.

15. FM 3-24/MCWP 3-33.5, pp. 5-14 to 5-17.

16. Stathis Kalyvas and Matthew Kocher recommend this approach in their own work on civil conflict. See Stathis N. Kalyvas and Matthew Kocher, "Violence and Control in Civil War: An Analysis of the Hamlet Evaluation System (HES)," unpublished manuscript presented at the annual meeting of the American Political Science Association, Philadelphia, August 27, 2003.

17. The author took part in such efforts while on the staff of the Strategy, Plans, and Assessments directorate of the Multi-National Forces—Iraq headquarters in Baghdad from May to September 2008. Consensus on an appropriate framework for defining success proved impossible to achieve.

18. Rory Stewart, *The Prince of the Marshes (And Other Occupational Hazards of a Year in Iraq),* Orlando, FL: Harcourt Inc., 2006, pp. 46, 405.

19. Note that this choice violates a typical rule of thumb for case selection — avoiding selection based on the value of the dependent variable. However, this research does not purport to be drawing a random or representative sample from the full population of cases, nor will it draw deterministic conclusions based on the results of these case studies. As a result, for the purposes of this research, the need to observe variation in the dependent variable trumps the usual rationales for avoiding selection on the dependent variable.

# CHAPTER 2

## RAMADI (SEPTEMBER 2004 to JULY 2005)

This chapter presents a case study of U.S. operations in and around the city of Ramadi from September 2004 to July 2005. Its focus is on the U.S. Army's 2nd Brigade Combat Team of the 2nd Infantry Division (2/2ID) and its subordinate units during that time period. The case is presented in seven parts covering the following topics: 1) an overview of the background and major events of the case; 2) the role of ethnic and religious identity politics in the case; 3) counterinsurgent actions with respect to providing security; 4) counterinsurgent actions with respect to improving governance; 5) any efforts toward political agreements that address ethno-religious cleavages; 6) an assessment of the outcome of the counterinsurgency; and 7) a concluding discussion and evaluation of the case in the context of this monograph's questions and analytical framework.

## CASE BACKGROUND

### Ramadi and the Insurgency.

Ramadi is the capital and the largest city of Iraq's western Anbar province. It is located in the upper Euphrates river valley, situated mostly on the southern banks of the river, about 70 miles west of Baghdad. In 2004, the World Food Program estimated its population to be 456,853,[1] though the total likely declined from that level during the course of the violence that occurred during the time period of this case study. Ramadi's population is ethnically and religiously homogeneous, with Sunni Muslim Arabs comprising more than 90 percent of the population.

Founded in 1869, the city sits along the primary road and rail lines connecting Baghdad and the heart of Iraq with Jordan and points westward (see Figure 2-1). This location has long given Ramadi an important commercial role, in both legitimate and illicit economic activity, and it also became a major transit point for foreign insurgents entering Iraq to fight U.S. and Iraqi security forces.

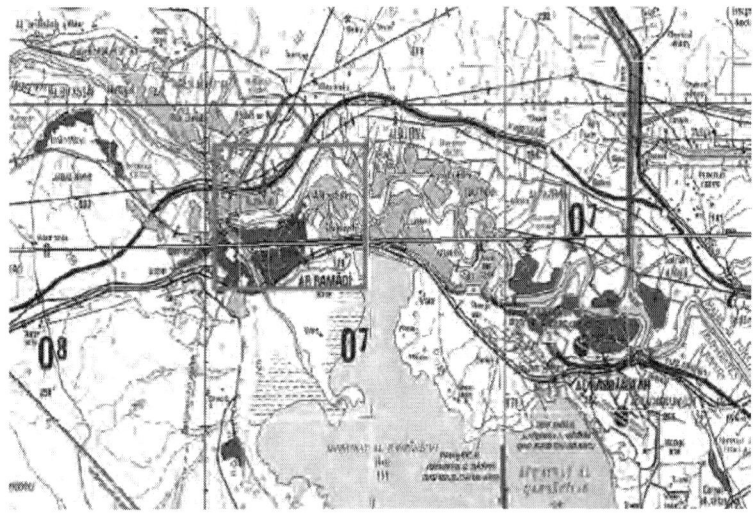

**Figure 2-1. Ramadi and Surrounding Area.[2]**

In part due to its role as a hub for international trade and transit, Ramadi has been a somewhat more cosmopolitan and secular city than its Anbar neighbors, such as Fallujah. It is the home of Anbar University, and has been a relatively liberal center for intellectual and cultural life.[3] Ramadi witnessed large scale demonstrations against Saddam Hussein in 1995, a phenomenon virtually unheard of in other Sunni Arab portions of Iraq.

At the same time, however, Ramadi was also home to many Ba'ath party officials, and the local and provincial government hierarchies in Ramadi were closely tied to Saddam Hussein's regime. The city served as the hub of Saddam's turbulent but largely successful program of co-opting the support of Anbar's tribal leaders,[4] and was also home to the Iraqi Army's combat engineers,[5] its special forces,[6] and a large number of active and retired senior officers. Consequently, the Coalition Provisional Authority's (CPA) Orders, numbers 1 and 2, banishing all Ba'ath party officials from office and disbanding the Iraqi Army, hit Ramadi especially hard.[7] Formerly powerful people in Ramadi had both the motivation and the tactical and technical expertise to mount an effective military opposition to the U.S. presence.

The insurgency in Ramadi was multifaceted and evolved over time, but generally comprised three overlapping groups. One U.S. battalion staff described the groups this way, using the labels most commonly used by the local population (and written in inimitable PowerPoint syntax):

- "Resistance - fighters who are resisting occupation by a foreign army; they fight the United States, and this is seen as an honorable endeavor; no central control of resistance groups.
- Terrorists - foreigners who are not from Ramadi, Al Anbar, or Iraq. There are locals who support Islamic extremist (global Salafi jihad/ Wahabbist) groups.
- Criminals - primary motivation is money, organized crime support both Terrorists and Resistance fighters."[8]

The staff also estimated that 25 percent of "resistance" fighters worked with the "terrorists." According to a civilian analyst working in Anbar during this period who conducted extensive interviews with insurgency supporters, "People always distinguished between the foreign jihadists and the Sunni nationalists, even though they tolerated the common cause that had been made between them."[9] However, the relative importance of the "resistance" and the "terrorists" shifted over time; specifically, al-Qaeda in Iraq (AQI) and its Islamic extremist compatriots gradually evolved from being the less important insurgent element of the two, to being the clearly predominant one.[10]

By September 2004, Ramadi was one of the hot spots of the insurgency, forming the southwestern corner of the so-called "Sunni Triangle" that extended to Baghdad in the east and Tikrit in the north. Though Fallujah was considered the center of the insurgency in Anbar, Ramadi was not far behind it in operational and strategic significance and in the intensity of combat. To cite just one indicator of this intensity, the brigade that 2/2ID replaced (the 1st Brigade Combat Team, 1st Infantry Division [1/1ID]) suffered more than 500 casualties, including 50 fatalities, during its tour from September 2003 to September 2004.[11] In just the 6 months prior to 2/2ID's arrival, the Marine battalion operating under 1/1ID that had the lone responsibility for the city of Ramadi (the 2nd Battalion, 4th Marine Regiment) suffered more than half of those casualties.[12]

## The Counterinsurgents.

During the period of this case study, the U.S. operational military headquarters in Iraq was known as Multi-National Corps-Iraq (MNC-I). Operations in Anbar province were overseen by Marine headquarters units, the 1st Marine Expeditionary Force (I MEF) and 1st Marine Division (1 MARDIV) until March 2005, then subsequently the 2nd Marine Expeditionary Force (II MEF) and 2nd Marine Division (2 MARDIV).

The 2/2ID, somewhat unusually, was an Army brigade operating under a Marine division-level headquarters. The brigade commanded 5,560 Soldiers, Marines, Airmen, and Sailors. Its main combat forces were three organic infantry battalions, one attached Marine infantry battalion, and an artillery battalion.[13]

The 2/2ID arrived in Ramadi at the end of August 2004 and officially took over responsibility for the battle space known as "AO [Area of Operations] Topeka" from 1/1ID on September 12. AO Topeka covered approximately 6,500 square kilometers of Ramadi and its surroundings, up to Lake Thar Thar in the north, Fallujah in the east, Hit in the west, and Lake Razazah in the south.[14]

The brigade deployed to Iraq (via Kuwait) directly from its home near the Korean Peninsula's demilitarized zone, where its mission and training had entirely focused on deterring and waging high-intensity conventional war against North Korea's armed forces. Apropos of this long-standing mission, the brigade's nickname was "Strike Force" and its motto was "Kill the Enemy!" (see Figure 2-2).

**Figure 2-2. 2/2ID Unit Insignia.[15]**

Like so many other Army units deploying to Iraq in the same period, 2/2ID had to prepare to deploy and re-orient its training and operating mindset on short notice, having received its deployment orders less than 3 months prior to its departure from Korea. After 11 months in Iraq, 2/2ID was relieved in place at the end of July 2005 by the 2nd Brigade Combat Team, 28th Infantry Division, from the Pennsylvania National Guard.

**What Happened (September 2004 to July 2005).**

Anbar province, after initially seeming ready to co-operate with Coalition forces immediately following the 2003 invasion, rapidly evolved into the main home of the Sunni insurgency. In the early days, U.S. forces in Ramadi, especially the Marine Corps, believed in the promise of showing a friendly face to the local population as a means of winning its loyalty.[16] As one reporter described:

> Commanders worked to instill sympathy for the local population through sensitivity training and exhortations from higher officers. Marines were ordered to

show friendliness through 'wave tactics,' including waving at people on the street.[17]

These attitudes proved short-lived, however, as attacks against U.S. forces quickly escalated in frequency and sophistication. In one particularly well-publicized and deeply felt incident in April 2004, a dozen Marines were killed in a single ambush in the city. Naturally, this environment hardened the attitudes of many U.S. forces, even those whose original intent had been to do what was necessary to win the hearts and minds of Ramadi residents. In the words of one Marine noncommissioned officer (NCO) who was deployed to Ramadi in the spring and summer of 2004, "My whole opinion of the people here has changed. There aren't any good people."[18] U.S. forces developed a strong sense that the general population was largely complicit in many insurgent attacks against them. Another Marine NCO relates the story of a rocket-propelled grenade attack on his platoon:

> When the Marines responded, the attacker fled, but they found that he had established a comfortable and obvious position to lie in wait. There, in an alleyway beside the shops was a seat and ammunition for the grenade launcher—along with a pitcher of water and a half-eaten bowl of grapes. . . . 'You could tell the guy had been hanging out all day. It was out in the open. Every single one of the guys in the shops could tell the guy was set up to attack us.'[19]

By the summer of 2004, U.S. forces were taking measures to reduce their disruptive effects on normal life in Ramadi, based on the premise that U.S. presence was an irritant and stoked some of the violence in the city. The Marine battalion there ceased patrolling the city almost entirely and instead set up observation posts throughout the city. But the change generated little improvement in the violence.[20] Indeed, the security situation had deteriorated to the point that the U.S. command was not confident it would be able to hold the planned January elections safely in the city.[21]

This period also witnessed the disintegration of what semblance of governmental authority had remained in the city. In August and September alone, Anbar's governor resigned after his sons were kidnapped and his own life was threatened,[22] the deputy governor was kidnapped and murdered,[23] and Ramadi's police chief was arrested by U.S. forces for having begun working with the insurgency. By late September, Anbar's beleaguered acting governor, who doubled as Ramadi's acting mayor, could only lament that, "We do not know who the attackers are or who is backing them. Are they backed from outside? Nobody knows."[24]

This was the environment in which 2/2ID took command of Ramadi in September. Commanders determined not to let Ramadi "become another Fallujah," where insurgents operated with impunity. Accordingly, 2/2ID took an aggressive early approach, launching three separate brigade-level offensive operations in its first 3 weeks in command.[25] These operations, according to a brigade press release, were designed to "deny anti-U.S. forces safe haven, round up suspected anti-U.S. leaders and exploit weapons caches used against legitimate forces in the area."[26] The tactics employed were mainly large-scale cordon-and-search operations.

These operations produced some results in terms of detained suspects and confiscated weapons, and yet seemed to have little effect on the level or intensity of attacks against U.S. forces. On a day-to-day basis,

U.S. forces in Ramadi had their hands full simply securing the city's main east-west road, known to the Americans as Route Michigan, and maintaining safe resupply of their own bases.[27]

By late October, 2/2ID had already suffered 12 Soldiers killed in action,[28] and the leader of Anbar's dominant Dulaym tribe declared that "the city is chaotic. There's no presence of the Allawi [federal] government." A Marine civil affairs NCO said: "We hit the deck one and a half months ago, and the area has changed for the downhill very quickly."[29]

In the face of this deteriorating situation, 2/2ID commander, Colonel Gary Patton, decided to realign his forces. Up until that point, only one of the brigade's four attached infantry battalions, the 2nd Battalion, 5th Marine Regiment (2/5 Marines), was based inside Ramadi. The other battalions were based in the areas immediately surrounding the city, including two full battalions in Ramadi's eastern suburbs. With approval from the division headquarters, Patton moved one of those two battalions, 1st Battalion, 503rd Infantry (1/503rd), from the east into the city, effectively doubling the number of U.S. combat forces inside Ramadi.

Before the increased troop levels could show much of an effect on security in Ramadi, however, operations in the city were overshadowed by the preparation and execution of the Coalition's major November assault on nearby Fallujah. Ramadi saw an increase in attacks as insurgents pulling back from Fallujah sought refuge or transit there. U.S. operations focused on shielding the city from these collateral effects, with only partial success. An Al Jazirah reporter described the situation in Ramadi on November 17 this way:

Life inside the city has completely stopped, and shops are closed. For several weeks now, students have not gone to schools and colleges. Electricity has been out for eight days. The U.S. forces entered the city from the western side trying to reach the eastern neighborhoods; they, however, were confronted by the fierce resistance of gunmen. Eyewitnesses said that fires blazed in several parts of the city due to the shootout, and warplanes are flying over.[30]

In the aftermath of the so-called "second battle of Fallujah," security conditions actually improved in Ramadi, and in December and January, the city began to show some signs of a return to normal life. By this time, the focus of U.S. operations had shifted to ensuring the relatively peaceful implementation of national elections at the end of January 2005. Much was at stake strategically with the elections as evidence of Iraq's democratic transition, and the participation of Anbar province's Sunni Arab population seemed particularly important. "From a symbolic and a political standpoint, conducting a successful election in Ramadi, the provincial capital, is critical," remarked Brigadier General Joseph Dunford, the assistant commander of the 1st Marine Division.[31]

Ultimately, election day in Ramadi produced both good and bad news for the United States. No major attacks occurred, which was both a surprise and a major victory for the security forces in the city. Turnout, however, was extremely paltry. Province-wide, turnout was only 2 percent, and early unofficial figures in Ramadi showed that only 1,700 of the city's 400,000 residents voted.[32] Intimidation by insurgents was a major factor in the low turnout, as was grave suspicion of the legitimacy and reliability of the process.

Even the Ramadi director of the Independent Electoral Commission of Iraq resigned, together with his staff, a few days before the elections due to death threats.[33]

In the wake of the elections, U.S. forces launched a new offensive throughout the upper Euphrates river valley, known as Operation RIVER BLITZ. In Ramadi, this effort was marked by the establishment of checkpoints at the main entrances to the city, as well as a curfew from 8 p.m. to 6 a.m.[34] The checkpoints helped to limit insurgents' freedom of movement,[35] though they were also manpower intensive[36] and drew some complaints from local residents for impeding commerce and daily life.[37] By April, 2/2ID was claiming some success for these measures, crediting them with "a drastic decline in the amount of insurgent activity."[38]

The late winter and spring of 2005 also saw a growing role for Iraqi security forces in Ramadi. Up to this point, efforts to shift responsibility for security to local forces had been almost entirely fruitless. The local police force mostly disintegrated in the fall, the Iraqi Army was not present, and a unit of the Iraqi National Guard, recruited largely from the local population, had disbanded in November due to its being completely ineffectual and compromised by the insurgents. But by the spring, some Iraqi Army units had deployed to Ramadi. In most cases, these units were a double-edged sword in terms of working with the local population. Most of the Army units were majority Shi'a Arab. Most of the soldiers were not happy to be in Anbar, and many Ramadi residents resented their presence, even interpreting it as a validation of their suspicions about American complicity in a Shi'a takeover of Iraq. These concerns were exacerbated further with the appointment in 2005 of Bayan Jabr Sulagh as the Minister of the Interior. Jabr was widely thought to be affiliated with the sectarian Badr Corps militia and soon gained a reputation for using elements of the national police to conduct ethnic cleansing.[39]

On the other hand, many of the Iraqi Army units, especially over time, proved capable of professionalism and avoidance of overtly sectarian behavior.[40] Their effectiveness in understanding the local environment, developing intelligence, and identifying insurgents was naturally far superior to that of the Americans.[41]

Importantly, the early months of 2005 also brought the first signs of an emerging rift between Ramadi's tribal leaders and the Islamist insurgents operating in the area, especially AQI. Some of the earliest evidence of a split came in the execution of seven foreign AQI members in retaliation for the assassination of a Dulaimi clan leader and Iraqi National Guard commander, Lieutenant Colonel Sulaiman Ahmed Dulaimi.[42] This was near the same time that reports surfaced of U.S. military officials as well as the Iraqi Defense Minister holding secret meetings with elements of the insurgency.[43] Unnamed sources told Al Jazirah that as a result of some of these meetings, "a military unit will be formed in the city of Al-Ramadi to preserve security. The unit will consist of former Iraqi army personnel and commanders and will not take orders from the U.S. forces or the Iraqi Defense Ministry. . . ."[44] At the same time, U.S. forces in the far western deserts of Anbar had just begun working with the Albu Mahal Desert Protectors, a tribally-based militia formed to combat AQI.[45]

Notwithstanding these developments, however, the United States faced a major obstacle in attempting to exploit the emerging hostility between groups of erstwhile insurgent allies—namely, its own policy.

As a rule, the United States remained extremely leery of creating local militias with no formal ties to the Iraqi government. After all, this was essentially the model that was attempted in handing off authority to the "Fallujah Brigade" in April 2004, an experiment generally viewed inside and outside the Coalition as a disastrous failure.[46] Instead, the United States was still hoping to marry up the local legitimacy enjoyed by Anbar's tribal leaders with the formal institutions of the Iraqi government, in particular the Iraqi Army. Bing West, a writer, former Marine, and former Pentagon official who spent many months in Anbar province during this period provides a stark illustration of this policy in action:

> The sheikhs offered a deal in March of 2005. They wanted arms and ammunition, plus vehicles. They would protect their turfs with a tribal force of roughly 5,000 men. They would agree to boundaries and point out the takfiris [Islamic extremists]. That would stop the IED attacks along the main roads. [Assistant commander of 1 MARDIV, Brigadier General Joseph] Dunford refused. You have an elected national government, he said, with a new army. Send your tribal sons to [the Army training center in] Taji. . . . Asked if he could promise they would return to their tribal areas, Dunford said no. There was an elected government and no need for another militia. The days of the tribes were over.[47]

Dunford went on to explain:

> In the spring of 2005, I met with dozens of sheikhs. They were shaken up by what we had done in Fallujah. They said they'd fight on our side, but refused to go through the government in Baghdad. In 2005, we weren't willing to accept that deal.[48]

In part because of this gap between the tribes and the United States, relationships between U.S. forces and the local population in Ramadi continued to develop slowly. 2/2ID did begin to make progress in identifying some local leaders in and around the city who were willing to work with them in trying to re-establish governance in the city, and the U.S.'s local intelligence networks slowly expanded.[49] At the same time, though, the local population continued to bristle at the restrictions imposed by U.S. forces. AQI attacks and intimidation continued to undermine efforts to stabilize the city. In May, the new Anbar governor was kidnapped in Ramadi and found dead a few weeks later.[50] AQI also aggressively targeted the growing number of sheikhs who appeared willing to challenge its strong influence. A new city council was just formed as 2/2ID prepared to depart the country in July 2005.

Unclassified statistics on overall attack trends in Ramadi during this period are not yet available. Anecdotal evidence is mixed, with some participants identifying reduced violence between the beginning and the end of 2/2ID's tour and some identifying roughly similar levels at the beginning and end of the period. Estimates of casualties suffered by 2/2ID and its subordinate units range from 68 to 98 killed in action with approximately 700 more wounded.[51]

What does seem clear, however, is a sharp deterioration in security in Ramadi subsequent to 2/2ID's departure. A few journalistic accounts chart the city's downward spiral. From August 2005:

> Insurgents in Anbar province . . . are fighting the U.S. military to a standstill. After repeated major offensives in Fallujah and Ramadi, . . . many U.S. officers and enlisted men have stopped talking about winning a

military victory in Iraq's Sunni Muslim heartland. . . Today, the street [in Ramadi] is pocked with holes left by bombs intended for U.S. convoys, storefronts are ripped by shrapnel, bullet holes tattoo walls, buildings have been blown to rubble by U.S. missile strikes and insurgent mortar volleys, and roofs are caved in by U.S. bombing. At the main U.S. base in Ramadi, artillery booms every night, sending more shells to pound insurgent positions in and around the city.[52]

From October 2005:

[In Ramadi,] Sunni Arab insurgents are waging their fiercest war against American troops, attacking with relative impunity just blocks from Marine-controlled territory. Every day, the Americans fight to hold their turf in a war against an enemy who seems to be everywhere but is not often seen. The cost has been high: in the last 6 weeks, 21 Americans have been killed here, far more than in any other city in Iraq and double the number of deaths in Baghdad . . . more than 2 years after the American invasion, this city of 400,000 people is just barely within American control. The deputy governor of Anbar was shot to death on Tuesday; the day before, the governor's car was fired on. There is no police force. A Baghdad cellphone company has refused to put up towers here. American bases are regularly pelted with rockets and mortar shells, and when troops here get out of their vehicles to patrol, they are almost always running.[53]

From December 2005:

It is clear that the U.S. forces are not present inside the city . . . there are no Iraqi forces either. Gunmen have assumed full control of the city. There is intensive shelling of the governorate building, the citizenship affairs building, which the U.S. forces use as their headquarters, and the main headquarters west of the city . . .[54]

It was only in late 2006 that Ramadi became the focal point of the Tribal Awakening that transformed the counterinsurgency in Anbar.

## Were Ethno-Religious Identity-Based Cleavages Significant?

Having experienced many generations in power, Iraq's Sunni Arab community has come to view political power as an important element of its identity. As one recent study of Anbar's tribes reported:

> The modern Sunni Arabs of Iraq take a great deal of pride in their religious and political history. They tend to regard themselves as the descendents and heirs to a long history of intellectual development, wealth, and political rule over the massive Islamic empire. They regard other ethnic and religious groups throughout the history of Iraq as less worthy of political power and influence.[55]

One commonly noted manifestation of this sense of political identity is that so many Sunni Arab Iraqis dispute the generally accepted population estimates that show Shi'a Arabs with a clear majority of Iraq's population. This view is not limited to the poor and uneducated, but is shared by many Sunnis who are wealthy, educated, well-traveled, and even pro-Western.[56]

Given this context, it is difficult to overstate the sense of disenfranchisement felt by many Sunni Arabs following the U.S. invasion in 2003. Even Sunni opponents of Saddam Hussein who welcomed the invasion and the change of regime were extremely upset by the influence granted to Shi'a exiles — pro-Western and pro-Iranian alike — in the Iraqi Governing Council and subsequently the Iraqi Interim Government.[57] Beyond the chagrin of coming up short in the division of spoils, Iraq's Sunni Arabs found the new political arrangement to be unnatural and a transgression of cultural norms. As noted at the beginning of this paper, a Sunni tribal leader captured this feeling well in his assertion that, Shi'a "cannot take charge of Iraq in the same manner as the Sunnis. The [Shi'a] are backwards. They are barbarian savages, they do not know true religion, theirs is twisted, it is not the true religion of Muhammad."[58]

In Ramadi, this sense of sectarian disenfranchisement was not the only driver of the insurgency, of course, but it was clearly one of the most important factors. While Ramadi, itself, is very homogeneous, one of its people's primary grievances was a view of the new Iraqi federal government as a sectarian Shi'a force, with the Iraqi Army and the Coalition serving as agents of that sectarian force. As a home to many Ba'athists and military officers, Ramadi in particular struggled to come to terms with the idea of an Iraq where its influence was weak.

The counterinsurgency expert John Nagl, who was a brigade operations officer in AO Topeka during 2003-04, just prior to 2/2ID's deployment, recalled:

> [We] came to realize that a very high percentage of the population—almost exclusively Sunni in our AO—did support the objectives of the insurgency, which was a restoration of Sunni ascendancy over the Shi'a. The Sunnis saw the American occupation as propping up the Shi'a and therefore targeted us. We couldn't win this fight at the local level. Success demanded national-level reconciliation between the Sunnis and the Shi'a. . . .[59]

According to Lieutenant Colonel Justin Gubler, battalion commander of the 1/503rd Infantry:

> Ramadi residents' biggest fear was being repressed and abused by the Shi'a government, and that was the biggest obstacle toward their working with us. We heard that from the sheikhs and from professionals and from former military officers. We were the ones that installed the Shi'a government, which they knew would mistreat them the way the Ba'ath party mistreated the Shi'a.[60]

Gubler's executive officer, Major Greg Sierra, said simply, "the Sunnis just weren't ready to play in the new Iraq — they hadn't accepted that things were going to be different."[61]

One commonly cited Sunni complaint was a belief that Iraq was being handed over to Iran. Just prior to the national elections in January 2005, the 1st Marine Division's commander, Major General Richard Natonski, toured polling stations. A group of Iraqi men gathered to describe their views to the general. One man told him "the election will only create a Shiite Muslim-dominated government in Baghdad that will ignore Sunni Muslim cities like Ramadi."[62] On election day, a professor told an American reporter that he was boycotting the election because he believed that it would be manipulated by pro-Iranian Shiite politicians. "Iraq will become part of Iran after this. I want no part of it."[63] Another Ramadi resident pleaded with a Marine intelligence officer at one point, "Don't leave us with this Iranian army."[64] Shortly after the elections, insurgent leaders told U.S. representatives in secret meetings that they saw the Shi'a-dominated government as being controlled by Iran and that their "aim was to establish a political identity that can represent disenfranchised Sunnis."[65]

It is telling that Ramadi remained among the most obstinate of the Sunni-dominated areas in coming to terms with participation in the national government. In the fall of 2005, the U.S. headquarters in Baghdad was claiming progress in bringing Sunnis into the political process. They cited public opinion survey results from June 2005 showing that majorities of Sunnis in most areas, including approximately 80 percent of Sunnis in Baghdad, believed that boycotting the January elections had been a "bad idea." But in Ramadi, only 40 percent believed the boycott had been a bad idea, while 46 percent still described the boycott as a "good idea."[66]

Other evidence of significant sectarian cleavages can be found in the reactions of Ramadi residents in the first half of 2005 to the increased deployment of largely Shi'a security forces to the area. One Shi'a Iraqi soldier in Ramadi commented, "Of course they don't like us. They don't like people from the south, so when we search them, they make faces at us." Another called Ramadi hostile territory, complaining that "it is a problem that we are Shiite. [The local people] think we are all spies." Naturally, insurgents exploited these tensions to maximum effect, distributing literature and graffiti referring to the Shi'a Army units as "rapists," "Jews," and "dogs of the Americans."[67]

For all the importance of sectarian Sunni identity in Ramadi, it is important to note that the salience of this identity was to some degree eclipsed by tribal identities. These identities overlapped heavily due to the city's homogeneity, but political identification and loyalties in Ramadi did tend to adhere more to tribal hierarchies than to religious ones, per se. As one intelligence officer described it, "the tribal identity trumped everything. It gives the leaders legitimacy."[68]

The strength of tribal identities and loyalties tended to be more pronounced in the surrounding areas than in the city, itself, where tribes intermixed.[69]

It is also important to note the weakness of Iraqi national identity that might otherwise have mitigated some of the divisive effects of strong tribal and sectarian identification. Several interviewees noted the absence of any Iraqi nationalism in Ramadi, except of the sort tied to Saddam Hussein's regime. For example, Colonel David Clark, the commander of the 1st Battalion, 506th Infantry Regiment (1/506th), commented that "The Iraqis that we knew and worked with were three or four things before they were Iraqis—clan, tribe, religion, all before they were Iraqis. Those interests came first, all above the national interest."[70]

In sum, it is clear that despite the absence of much sectarian violence in Ramadi, conflict between Iraq's Sunni and Shi'a Arabs was quite central to the origins and evolution of the insurgency there.

## Were Good Security Operations Conducted?

Evaluating the quality of U.S. security operations during this period is not simple. The record is mixed and complex. Several interviewees felt that a "conventional" mindset prevailed in the brigade for too long. This mindset manifested itself in 2/2ID's planning and operations in an emphasis on targeting of insurgents rather than population security. "We were too kinetic, too focused on offensive operations," said one officer. "There was a tendency toward focusing on raids, killing and capturing bad guys, etc."[71] A reporter embedded with the brigade commented that "U.S. forces were still in Cold War mode—they were all about fighting and killing . . . there were a lot of raids, detentions and the like that alienated the populace."[72]

This view, though not universal among the interviewees, was common up and down the chain of command. Marine Corporal Peder Ell did not see great value in large offensive sweep operations, saying, "We'd pick up bad guys and disrupt their operations, but it only worked for a while. They would just come back in after the operation had ended."[73] Colonel Patton, the brigade commander, agreed: "We did a lot of those brigade-level and battalion-level ops and it never got us much of anything important. They were fruitless, and they pissed people off."[74] Besides alienating the local population, operations that involved raiding a lot of houses, arresting a lot of people, and taking away people's guns, also served to confirm some Anbaris' suspicions that the United States was making war on the whole community of Sunnis on behalf of the sectarian federal government.[75]

According to 2/2ID's artillery battalion commander, Lieutenant Colonel John Fant:

> It took us a long time to understand that this was not a brigade fight, it was a platoon and squad fight. I think our conventional training clouded our approach to the problem. . . . The brigade's role should be political and resource provision. . . .[76]

Yet these brigade roles were not consistently pursued. Another officer summarized the problem this way:

> What I ranked as important were developing governance and developing the Iraqi police and military. If you just looked at our resource allocation, though, you might assume that the main priority was killing bad guys. There was a lot of variation across different operating units and staff in terms of their relative focus on governance vs. kinetic operations. I don't think

we ever had a common picture across the AO of the center of gravity, whether it was the population or the enemy.[77]

Two other officers interviewed argued that the brigade leadership may have underestimated the importance of cultivating relationships with local leaders. One recalled an incident early in the brigade's deployment in which the commander cancelled consecutive meetings with a local leader who had had a relationship with the previous brigade commander, and then sent a lieutenant colonel to meet with him. In a culture that places a high value on seniority and respect, this officer believed, this approach "was an affront to [the leader] that set the tone for the whole time we were there." Like other interviewees, he attributed such mistakes in part to a "conventional mindset."[78] Another interviewee believed that the brigade commander "did not embrace his role as the person to lead engagement with the local leaders" until the latter half of the brigade's deployment.[79]

On the other hand, the brigade's focus on conventional combat operations was at least partly a result of the level of threat it faced nearly immediately upon its arrival in Ramadi. The fall of 2004 was "brutal, just really violent," said one officer.[80] In the words of Colonel Clark, the 1/506th commander, "We were up to our eyeballs fighting those guys, so we weren't able to concentrate on the political and social and economic aspects."[81] In this environment, traditional counterinsurgency approaches had difficulty taking root. Another officer offered this example:

> In the fall, we planned to set up a 'place of hope' in one neighborhood, where we were going to try to concentrate some security and reconstruction efforts. It was

essentially an ink spot approach, classic clear, hold, and build. We wrote the plan, but then as we were getting ready to execute the plan, one of our battalions got engaged in pretty heavy fighting and the decision got made that we're not going to implement the 'place of hope'. And I felt like this was a turning point when we turned away from the idea of focusing on securing the population.[82]

The serious challenges posed by the high threat level led some interviewees to reject the charge that the brigade had been "too kinetic."[83]

Another major limitation 2/2ID faced in establishing security for Ramadi's population was its relatively small number of troops. AO Topeka had over half a million people, and 2/2ID totaled only around 5,500 personnel. As with any modern military unit, a substantial number of those personnel were engaged in support functions and were not combat troops. Colonel Patton estimated that even after he moved an additional battalion into the city — a choice he called one of the best decisions he made during the deployment — there were only about 1,800 U.S. combat forces in Ramadi proper.[84] This means the United States had approximately one Soldier in the city for every 222 residents, a ratio more than four times smaller than the ratio the 2006 counterinsurgency field manual notes as a commonly-recommended "minimum force density" for effective counterinsurgency.[85] Representative of the many comments from interviewees on the subject of troop numbers is this assessment from a 2/5 Marines company commander, Captain Eric Dougherty:

The biggest problem was that we were so undermanned, that we couldn't give the people confidence that we'd be around. As soon as you're gone, the people could count on the insurgents to show up and intimidate them or punish them in retribution for their cooperation with the Coalition. That puts the population in a precarious position—they were waiting to see who would win before they picked a side.[86]

The natural solution to the problem of inadequate forces is augmentation with indigenous forces. Indeed, the development of Iraqi security forces was a key component of 2/2ID's operations. However, this proved to be problematic on two related levels. First, for most or all of 2/2ID's tenure in Ramadi, Iraqi security forces there were totally inadequate to the task of providing security. In the first half of the brigade's deployment, Iraqi security forces were virtually nonexistent. The police force was heavily infiltrated, unreliable, ill-equipped, and eventually quit en masse.[87] A local Iraqi National Guard brigade was entirely ineffective, partly due to a lack of training, but also due to systematic insurgents' intimidation of Guard soldiers' families. U.S. forces disbanded the brigade altogether in the fall of 2004.[88] There was some improvement over time, especially among Iraqi Army units deployed to Ramadi from other parts of Iraq during the spring of 2005.[89] But these units remained a weak supplement to the U.S. combat forces in the area.

The second related problem was that Coalition policy at the strategic level emphasized the importance of transition of authority and control to Iraqi forces, not population security. In the words of the Corps commander who took charge at MNC-I in January 2005, Lieutenant General John Vines, the goal was "rapid progress in training and preparing Iraqis to assume responsibility for security in every province."[90] Thus any U.S. officers advocating a greater focus on population security had not only the inadequacy of available resources to contend with, but also a policy that pointed in the opposite direction.

Perhaps inevitably in this environment, the approaches employed by U.S. forces in Ramadi varied by subordinate unit and in general improved over time. Brigade-level sweeps were eventually replaced by more small-unit patrolling, and the establishment of checkpoints, which provided a modicum of consistent presence in at least a few locations in the city.[91] This enabled units to improve their ability to collect intelligence and to build relationships with the local population to some degree. Even these adaptations were hamstrung, though, by the limited numbers of troops available. And it was only near the very end of 2/2ID's deployment that units began to refocus their intelligence collection efforts away from targeting and toward understanding the socio-political dynamics of the local population.[92]

Overall, this record returns a somewhat ambiguous answer to the question, "Were good security operations conducted?" From a strategic perspective, even allowing for variation and improvement over time described above, the variety of problems outlined here point to an answer closer to "no" than "yes."

### Was Good Governance Provided?

One of the distinguishing characteristics of Ramadi during this period was the thoroughgoing dysfunction of the government. Leaders of the provincial and local government and of the police were routinely targeted by insurgents for intimidation and assassination. Those who chose to continue to serve in the face of threats against them were often killed. Mayors, provincial governors, and police chiefs in Ramadi tended to have short tenures in office that ended in death, resignation, or arrest for participation in the insurgency.

Hence governance of any sort, good or otherwise, was a scarce commodity in Ramadi during 2004-05. Most interviewees stressed the severe limitations on reconstruction efforts that prevailed due to the violence and intimidation. Reconstruction projects were regularly attacked, and Iraqis who were seen or suspected of working with the United States or taking funding from them were threatened and murdered.[93] One interviewee, who did not want this story attributed, related the following illustration of the severity of this problem:

> One time, we detained a guy for two weeks, just so he could then go back out into the city and profess to have a major grievance against the U.S. as a cover for taking U.S. money and starting a sewer renovation project. That's how reluctant people were to be seen to take American money.

This dynamic was particularly damaging because it subverted not only U.S. reconstruction efforts and attempts to improve governance, but also efforts to provide jobs for Ramadi's thousands of unemployed military-age males. Interviewees differed on the extent to which unemployment was a cause of the insurgency, but there is no question that it facilitated recruitment for the insurgents.[94]

Insurgents also occasionally targeted civilian infrastructure, further suggesting a deliberate attempt to make the city ungovernable. For example, just in 2/2ID's first month in Ramadi, insurgents blew up an agricultural center and the Red Crescent office, and then blamed the attacks on U.S. forces.[95] Another obstacle to improving governance was corruption and a certain lack of civic culture. Colonel David Clark offered one of many examples:

> We spent a lot of money getting the water purification system rebuilt and operational, and we got that all set up—should have been a tremendous victory for the people. But before long, it shut down, why? Because the guards were stealing the gasoline for the engine and selling it on the black market. And all the people along the line were tapping into it and contaminated it.[96]

Shortcomings in the U.S.'s own capacity and planning also hampered governance-related initiatives. One Marine officer complained that:

> [T]here was very little done in the way of working with the government. . . . I never felt that there was a State Department presence or a [provincial reconstruction team]. . . . We had a civil affairs reservist in our battalion—his job was to coordinate the civil reconstruction efforts—it was totally ineffective, we couldn't get anything done because there was no supporting bureaucracy and no unified vision.[97]

The training of the brigade's staff and leadership was also quite limited regarding execution of infrastructure and civil planning projects.[98]

In spite of all these difficulties, there were some governance improvement successes, mostly on a relatively small scale. For example, 2/2ID ran a number of missions aimed at rebuilding infrastructure and providing humanitarian aid to the city's residents.[99] Projects included building medical clinics, soccer fields, refurbishing schools and Anbar University, expanding police stations, and restoring a badly damaged mosque.[100] A Marine company commander recalls an attempt to set up a model city in their area:

We never quite got there. But the idea was, how do we get to the future of Ramadi, so we envisioned a model city where everything was working the way it should be, with sanitation, education, security. . . . And we were also able to run some humanitarian aid . . . on the western side of the city. The local people in those areas loved it. They appreciated the help.[101]

Of the projects pursued, improving electrical power generation and distribution was prominent, and some slow progress was made in this area. Anbar province was receiving less than 8 hours per day of electric power as of May 2004, which was down from its pre-war standards of 9-15 hours per day.[102] By March 2006, Anbar had gone up to 12-16 hours per day.[103]

One measure of the U.S. level of activity in attempting to improve the quality of life in Ramadi can be found in the records of the Commander's Emergency Response Program (CERP). This program provides money that brigade commanders and their subordinate commanders can use at their discretion to meet local needs in their areas of operation. CERP spending typically, though not exclusively, goes to relatively small, relatively short-term projects, and is also used to pay reparations for property damaged in combat or to family members of killed and wounded civilians. In Ramadi, estimated CERP spending increased significantly over the months of this case study (see Figure 2-4). Estimated spending by quarter rose from $1.1 million (August-October) to $2.0 million (November-January) to $2.1 million (February-April) to $2.4 million (May-July).[104] This represents an increase from beginning to end of a factor of 2.2.

Some commanders in Iraq claim to have noted a pattern of declining violence in the wake of CERP spending, including Lieutenant General Peter Chiarelli, the MNC-I commander during 2006, and Colonel John Charlton, who commanded U.S. forces in the Ramadi area during 2007.[105] Charlton, who spent $87 million in CERP funds during 15 months in his area of operations, claimed that "We did more to win counterinsurgency with our CERP dollars than we did with our weapons."[106] However, there is reason to question the causal link between CERP spending and violence.

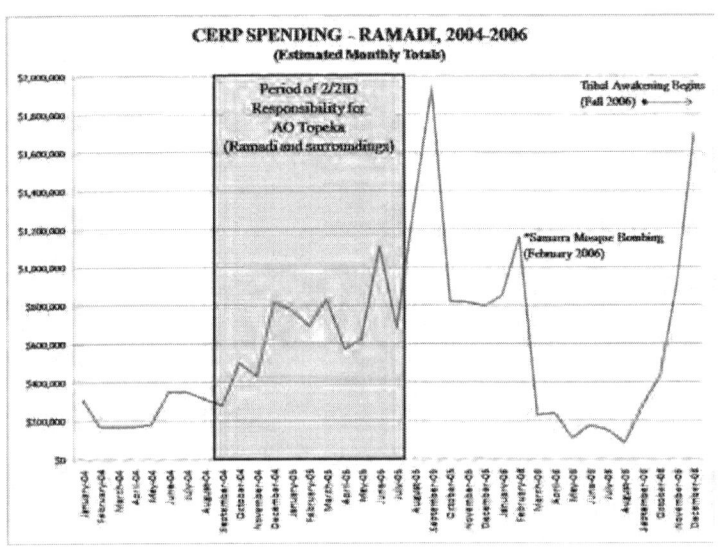

**Figure 2-3. Estimated Monthly CERP Spending in Ramadi.**

In the first multivariate statistical analysis conducted on district-level Iraq data,[107] Eli Berman, Jacob Shapiro, and Joseph Felter found no significant relationship at all between CERP spending and insurgent violence through 2006. They do find some correlation between the two factors starting in 2007, so their work perhaps qualifies Charlton's statement rather than contradicts it.

One specific example that suggests a complicated causal relationship between spending and security is one of Charlton's own reconstruction success stories, a glass and ceramics factory that Charlton's forces invested in heavily and got up and running in Ramadi in 2007. CERP was clearly not the decisive factor in this success story, because the United States spent over half a million dollars in CERP funds across 11 different contracts on that same glass factory during 2005 without it ever opening.[108] Only after Anbar's Tribal Awakening began in the fall of 2006 did the spending begin to have its intended effect.

Charlton's comments, themselves, also reveal a certain degree of ambivalence about the direction of causation with regard to CERP spending and changes in violence levels. On the one hand, he asserted that ". . . the results [of CERP] were clearly evident on the ground. Attacks in my area went from 30-35 per day down to essentially zero." But he also argued that "The key to any type of reconstruction or stabilization project is to establish a secure environment first. . . . Once we had [that], we were then able to work with the Iraqis to rebuild."[109]

This kind of confusion is common, and reflects one of counterinsurgency's classic recurring dilemmas discussed in the first chapter — that security is a pre-requisite for good governance while good governance is a pre-requisite for security. For some interviewees, this dilemma resonated with their experience in Ramadi.

Other interviewees questioned whether this dilemma was, in fact, at work in Ramadi. Without exception, they believed in the dependency of good governance on some threshold level of security. But some doubted the necessary causal link in the opposite direction, suggesting that Ramadi residents' attitude toward U.S. forces and the local government was far more linked to security than to any other aspect of governance. In fact, some interviewees reported indifference among the population about demonstrations of good governance—the people were far more interested in reliable security.[110] 2/2ID's commander commented that:

> Security was first and foremost what people wanted. That was the feedback we always got. . . . We gave the hospital medical supplies, conducted road repair, installed trash receptacles. But basically, this stuff couldn't take root while we were there—it didn't do any good coming from us—it had to come from the government. So for us, these things didn't end up making critical contributions to the fight.[111]

This observation came not only from U.S. forces, but also from local leaders. For example, the acting governor of Anbar and mayor of Ramadi in October complained, "The marines are not protecting us. It's true that they've helped us with some projects such as improving the water supply and sewage disposal and rebuilding schools. But people think all that is worthless. They need security."[112]

Moreover, even measures that were having some positive effects on security were viewed with hostility by some of the local population. In May 2005, some Ramadi residents staged a "sit-in" to highlight their grievances against U.S. forces. According to Al-Sharqiyah television news, Ramadi "looked completely empty and paralyzed this morning with the start of a 2-day sit-in in protest against the U.S. forces' practices against its residents." Protesters "called for ending the siege imposed on the city for 2 months, the departure of the U.S. forces from the city, the release of prisoners, stopping the acts of harassment against the residents of Al-Ramadi, putting an end to raid operations against citizens' houses, and stopping indiscriminate shooting."[113] Whatever the validity of these particular complaints, it was clear that the United States had a very high bar to clear in establishing any modicum of legitimacy for its governance activities in the city. Overall, it appears that good governance generally remained beyond the reach of the counterinsurgents in Ramadi during this time period.

## Were Political Agreements Addressing Ethno-Religious Cleavages Pursued?

Two major cleavages defined the insurgency in Anbar and Ramadi during 2004-05. The first was between the Sunni Arabs and the new government of Iraq. The second was between those Sunni Arabs and the U.S.-led Coalition. These two cleavages were closely related since, as noted above, many Anbaris saw the U.S. forces as working in concert with a Shi'a-led federal government. To a significant degree, this perception was correct—the United States was very clearly in concert with the new Iraqi federal government. The United States would have categorically rejected the characterization of that government as "Shi'a-led" or as sectarian in any other way. Nevertheless, the U.S. policies were based on a fundamental premise that the institutions of the new Iraqi government were the sole instruments of legitimate political power in the new Iraq.

Proceeding from this premise, U.S. policy from the establishment of the CPA at least through the period of this case study was to insist that U.S. cooperation with tribal sheikhs and other nongovernmental power brokers was contingent on the integration of these groups into the security and governance mechanisms of the federal government. In 2003, Anbar CPA representative Keith Mines lobbied to create a *loya jirga*, or tribal council, to negotiate the distribution of political power in the new Iraq or, failing this, to at least empower the sheikhs who came forward to support the United States. But the CPA leadership had no interest in this, being ever fearful of empowering nongovernmental militias and hence undermining the larger state-building effort.[114] As one intelligence officer working in Iraq in 2003 put it, "the standard answer we got from Bremer's people was that tribes are a vestige of the past, that they have no place in the new democratic Iraq."[115]

This policy then served as a major stumbling block to negotiating any sort of political compromise with local leaders in Ramadi. Colonel Clark acknowledged that, "it would have been way outside the box for us to accept [tribal overtures for creation of militias] at that time. It was against the policy, and it would have been difficult to predict how large the phenomenon was going to be."[116] General Joseph Dunford's comments cited earlier in this chapter neatly summarize the situation: "[The sheikhs] said they'd fight on our side, but refused to go through the government in Baghdad. In 2005, we weren't willing to accept that deal."[117] The 1st Marine Division commander concurred and defended this view: "The problem we had with local militias was that they did not work. The Fallujah Brigade is an example. So I don't think this kind of initiative would have succeeded in 2005. It wasn't a missed opportunity at all."[118] This same reluctance continued to prevail under II MEF, which took over control of U.S. operations in Anbar province in March 2005. The limitations of this policy were certainly not mitigated by the 2/2ID leadership's previously noted slowness in embracing its role in engaging local leaders.

This is not to suggest that U.S. leaders were unaware of or unwilling to address the sectarian grievances of the Anbari Sunnis more generally. MEF commanders did pursue several initiatives to try to bridge the gap between Anbar and the federal government, such as achieving better Sunni representation in Baghdad, moderating de-Ba'athification, and advocating a greater role for Sunni officers in the Iraqi Army.[119] But the effects of such efforts were hampered so long as the United States held the tribes' claims to having their own legitimacy at arm's length. This attitude tended to reinforce the common cause between the local resistance and the Islamist extremists. The 1/503rd commander, Lieutenant Colonel Gubler, explained the problem this way:

> For Sunnis, the fledgling Iraqi government can be seen to rely on illegitimate security forces—the U.S. and/or Shi'a militias. Hence, as the [Iraqi Army] becomes larger and more effective as a security force, the less likely it is that the Shi'a government will negotiate a power-sharing deal with the Sunnis.[120]

For the first several months of 2/2ID's tenure in Ramadi, seeking local leaders who were willing to work with the Coalition and were also not working with the insurgents was a challenge. A Marine company commander who left Ramadi in March lamented that, "We never really nailed down who the real power brokers were. We dealt with the provincial government, but they weren't the guys who were pulling the strings."[121]

As the split between AQI and the tribes began to open, however, opportunities to work with tribal leaders began to present themselves to the United States during the spring and summer of 2005. Effective response to these opportunities was slow, given the difficulty of even distinguishing real leaders from charlatans and profit-seekers (so-called "fake sheikhs"[122]). But over time, beginning at company and battalion levels, the United States began to build some relationships with sheikhs who showed promise as potential allies. As it became clear that the U.S. forces were not leaving the city, even some sheikhs who had been working with the insurgency seemed interested in seeking some accommodation with the U.S. Colonel Patton described the evolution of his own thinking on this point:

> The real power base in Ramadi was in the tribes, so if we were going to make any inroads in governance, we figured out that we would have to work through the sheikhs and the tribes. That wasn't something that we understood on day one, it took us time to figure that out... Why did it take so long to get to this realization? Because we were trying to work through the government and were not enthusiastic about propping up centers of power outside government channels.[123]

By the summer, 2/2ID units had developed a sheikh security council comprising two dozen sheikhs.[124] Still, these relationships proceeded fitfully, with a few steps forward often matched by a few steps back. For example, some tribal leaders in the 1/503rd's AO requested that the United States lift its checkpoints and extend the evening curfew by a couple hours. The United States forces complied, but that resulted in violence immediately rising again. The battalion's executive officer reports:

At that point, in June, several of the tribal leaders planned a major meeting when they were going to get everyone together to discuss and coordinate their actions as part of a new effort to oppose the insurgents. We were prohibited from attending this meeting because they were going to great lengths to avoid their efforts being seen as associated with us. But al Qaeda knew what they were doing, they assassinated guys, and scared them away, so the meeting didn't even happen.[125]

Carter Malkasian, a civilian analyst at the I MEF headquarters, cited such setbacks in tribal organization against AQI as evidence that in 2005, the environment was not yet ready for a major shift. He suggests, "Maybe what was happening was that the leadership had started to change its views, but the majority of the insurgents — the foot soldiers — were still committed to the cause."[126]

In parallel with trying to cultivate tribal allies, development of a city council became a key focus for the 2/2ID brigade staff beginning in the spring of 2005. One of the principal challenges of this effort was simply identifying who would be amenable to gathering to discuss issues. Eventually, this effort did bear fruit, and a city council had just formed when the brigade turned over control of the city to its successor.[127] Even so, there remained a critical gap between the authority exercised by the official government and by the tribal leaders. Colonel Patton explains:

The provincial and city governments that were just starting to function were not especially pleased with the tribal leaders' influence. We knew that bridging this gap was the end game, but basically, the sheikhs controlled a lot more people and resources than the nearly absent government did.[128]

Some interviewees viewed these early in-roads into tribal alliance building as the earliest roots of what would become the Tribal Awakening movements the following year.[129]

On balance, though, in spite of these early instances of building relationships with the city's tribal leaders, the evidence suggests that during the period of this case study, the United States was not able to pursue any serious political agreements that would address the fundamental sectarian cleavage between the disenfranchised Sunnis of Ramadi and the new Iraqi government. U.S. policy at the strategic level resisted the avenues of political compromise that were most salient to that cleavage, and the need to move in this direction only became clear gradually to counterinsurgents at the operational and tactical levels.

### Was the Counterinsurgency Successful?

The outcomes of the counterinsurgency over the course of 2/2ID's deployment are mixed. If success is measured only by attack statistics over the course of the brigade's 10 ½ months in command in Ramadi, then some degree of success is discernible. Unclassified attack data is sparse, though the 1/503rd's executive officer reported that attacks in the eastern half of the city went from 10 per day to 2-3 per day over those 10 ½ months.[130]

After returning to the United States, that battalion's leadership noted a variety of improvements in their area of operations, as shown in Table 2-1.[131]

| September 2004 | July 2005 |
|---|---|
| • Enemy contact everyday—Direct fire (RPG, RPK, PKM) and indirect fire (rocket and mortar) <br> • People did not go into the street, to work, school, or market <br> • People scared and refused to talk to or support U.S. forces <br> • No ISF; IPs worked with the enemy <br> • Electricity was intermittent <br> • No running water in half the city <br> • Sewers clogged and trash was piled in the city | • Enemy contact less than once per week—IED/SVBIED or indirect fire <br> • Main supply route (MSR) Michigan remained 'BLACK' <br> • Life normalized—People drove and walked on the streets; children played, schools, markets, and businesses were open <br> • People felt safer and tolerated or supported CF <br> • ISF present; IP units were forming. <br> • Electricity restored to the city; Power outages 2-3 times per week <br> • Running water to all the city <br> • Sewers were unclogged and trash was picked up routinely |

**Table 2-1. Changes in Eastern Ramadi, September 2004-July 2005.**

The brigade reported a somewhat more modest list of 10 "Brigade Achievements" in the unclassified portion of its own After Action Report:[132]

1. Executed a historic deployment from Korea into a combat zone.

2. No serious heat casualties during the entire deployment.

3. Supported and participated in combat operations in Fallujah, preventing Ramadi from becoming a second insurgent stronghold.

4. Provided a secure voting environment in Ramadi for the January 30 national elections.

5. Local leader engagement facilitated the formation of a Ramadi city council and multi-agency security council.

6. Re-enlisted over 800 Soldiers in combat.

7. Enabled 99 percent of 2BCT [2nd Brigade Combat Team] Soldiers to participate in the R&R [rest and relaxation] leave program.

8. Developed and employed five new Iraqi Army battalions, and built/renovated six new Iraqi Army compounds.

9. Captured or killed over 2,100 insurgents.

10. Captured a brigade-equivalent amount of weapons and resources.

The only achievement on the list that resembles something like strategic success—the claim of preventing Ramadi from becoming a "second insurgent stronghold"—was always a close-run thing, and proved to be quite fragile in the months following the brigade's departure.

Interviewees expressed a wide range of views on how successful their mission had been. Of 16 interviewees who answered a question about the success or failure of the mission, five characterized it as success. Interestingly, four of those five were Marines who left Ramadi in March 2005. One called the mission a failure. Ten interviewees felt that 2/2ID had achieved something in between success and failure. The following two quotes are representative of that view. From 1/503rd executive officer Major Greg Sierra:

> Was this success in counterinsurgency or just success in combat ops? Even though we had multiple lines of effort, it was almost all combat ops. So even though we didn't manage to build much in terms of political and economic development, we did start to set the conditions, and helped lay the foundation for what happened later, in terms of working with the sheikhs.[133]

And from 2/2ID's artillery battalion commander, Lieutenant Colonel John Fant:

I've come to the conclusion that we just held the place in check. We may not have won, but we did prevent it from getting so out of control that it would require another Fallujah type operation. We resisted the overall collapse, and in some ways set the conditions for the brigades that followed to help develop the Awakening.[134]

Whatever degree of success the brigade achieved during its time in Ramadi, there is little doubt that it was short-lived. As shown earlier in the chapter, reports from Ramadi in fall of 2005 were relentlessly grim, depicting an environment as bad or worse as the one that had greeted 2/2ID upon its arrival in 2004. By March 2006, a Provincial Stability Assessment conducted jointly by the U.S. Embassy and Multi-National Force-Iraq (MNF-I) rated Anbar province as "critical" on a scale of stable, moderate, serious, and critical. This designation meant to signify the following characteristics:

- a government that is not functioning or has not formed, or that is only be [sic] represented by a single strong leader;
- an economy that does not have the infrastructure or government leadership to develop and is a significant contributor to instability; and,
- a security situation marked by high levels of [insurgent] activity, assassinations and extremism.[135]

Clearly, 2/2ID cannot be held responsible for the deterioration in Ramadi's security environment following its departure from the city. Without much more investigation, it is impossible to estimate how much of that deterioration resulted from changes in the environment or the insurgency itself, as opposed to changes in the U.S. policy or operations. Still, it seems fair to conclude, based on both the modesty and the evident fragility of the progress achieved by the United States during the period of this case study that the counterinsurgency mission was not successful in a strategic sense.

**Evaluation.**

Table 2-2 summarizes simple answers for the study's framework questions suggested by the evidence presented in this chapter. It is clear that identity-based cleavages were at the heart of the insurgency in Ramadi and Anbar province. Fundamental disagreement over the legitimacy of Sunni versus Shi'a Arab rule in Iraq and in Anbar was not the only source of conflict, but it was the most important among insurgents other than the religious extremists who flocked to the banner of al-Qaeda in Iraq. This problem was evident from the beginning of the conflict, and the evidence presented here confirms that this dynamic, while evolving, continued to prevail throughout the time period of this case study.

| Cases | Identity Cleavages | Good Security | Good Governance | Political Agreement | Success |
|---|---|---|---|---|---|
| Ramadi 2004-2005 | Yes | Ambiguous | No | No | No |

**Table 2-2. Case Study Variable Summary for Ramadi.**

It is also clear that as of mid-2005, the United States was not yet prepared to pursue political strategies that would directly address these cleavages. More precisely, the United States had staked everything on achieving a grand political bargain at the national level that should have addressed the grievances of Sunnis in Anbar. But as national-level reconciliation efforts remained bogged down, counterinsurgents in Anbar were left to fight their inherently political war with little discretion for addressing political grievances.

To say this is not necessarily to indict the policy choices made. U.S. leaders in Washington and Baghdad were loath to undermine the fragile sovereignty of the new Iraqi government by empowering tribal leaders in Anbar province. Moreover, as noted above, there were good reasons to doubt the viability of Sunni tribal groups fighting AQI effectively. The failed experiment with the Fallujah Brigade loomed large over proposals for arming tribal militias. In retrospect, the advantage of empowering the tribes is evident, but the risks of this strategy to the stability of the Iraqi state were significant.[136] Even so, should this case count as evidence in support of the general argument on the greater importance of identity politics relative to good governance?

Whatever support the case does provide must be qualified by the fact that the U.S. counterinsurgents do not score very highly on security operations or good governance in this case. With security, there is substantial evidence that 2/2ID's initial approach to fighting the insurgency through large cordon and search operations was unproductive at best and counterproductive at worst. The decision at strategic levels to allocate a single brigade combat team to a population center with around a half million people did not set 2/2ID up to succeed in its security mission. On the other hand, these negative factors were partially mitigated over time, first by 2/2ID's gradual adaptation to smaller scale operations with a growing focus on securing the population; and second, by the deployment of Iraqi security forces into the city. While these improvements appear to have been incremental and uneven, they belie an easy negative categorization of the quality of security operations for the case.

The coding of the good governance variable is more clear. Good governance cannot be said to have failed in this case, exactly; perhaps it is more accurate to say that it was barely attempted. By most accounts, U.S. forces believed in the potential value of improving governance in Ramadi, as signified, for example, by the growing CERP expenditures over time. But they were unable to make significant and sustained investments in this objective due to the persistent levels of insurgent violence and intimidation in the city.

So together, the weak contributions of security and governance in this case make the marginal impact of the political agreement variable on the outcome harder to isolate. Still, the causal link between U.S. policy in 2004 and 2005 of discouraging the legitimation of local Sunni tribes and the persistence of the insurgency in Ramadi during this period seems strong. Fundamentally, what institutions of governance existed in Ramadi at that time — principally the United States and, to a lesser degree, the Iraqi security forces — were perceived as illegitimate. This perception was not based on failures of performance, but rather on presumptions of inherent legitimacy tied to ethno-religious identity. So in this sense, this case does provide some evidence of the relative importance to counterinsurgency of political agreements addressing ethno-religious cleavages.

A relevant counterfactual question here would be, if the United States had managed to stand up a local government and provide a greater amount of infrastructure improvements, basic service provision, and economic development, would the insurgency have retained the strength that it did? The question is impossible to answer, though as described above, some interviewees were skeptical that more success in improving the quality of governance in the city would have had a great impact on the insurgency. In any case, the conditions that would probably have been necessary to allow for such a scenario seem almost categorically precluded by the prevailing political situation.

Perhaps the most compelling evidence of this interpretation of causal factors in Ramadi can be found in the Tribal Awakening developments there and elsewhere in Anbar in 2006-07. A more detailed investigation of the Awakening using this analytic lens awaits future research, but even its basic storyline is instructive for these purposes. In early 2006, the Coalition was already reporting some positive effects of the expanding split between Sunni rejectionists and jihadists among the insurgents.[137] AQI had continued to alienate Sunni Iraqis with its intolerance and intimidation. At the same time, the first instances of cooperation between U.S. forces and tribal groups were bearing fruit in al Qaim in the Western Anbar desert. Former insurgents began openly fighting each other. In February 2006, six insurgent groups, including the 1920s Brigades and the Islamic Movement for Iraq's Mujahideen, released a statement announcing a cooperative effort to form a people's cell to oppose AQI and to provide security in Anbar.[138]

Over the course of the next 1½ years, Ramadi transformed from "the blackest rat-hole in the dark insurgent sewer of the upper Euphrates valley," as David Kilcullen memorably called it, to a model for effective cooperation between the United States and the local Iraqi population. Attacks dropped from 100 a day to only a few.[139] The reasons for this transformation, of course, are numerous and complex. But improvements in the quality of governance in Ramadi or Anbar are conspicuously absent from the explanations offered by analysts and participants, alike.[140] Bing West dismisses the importance of such factors explicitly: "The Awakening wasn't attributable to economic development; Anbar was starved for funds. It wasn't due to enlightened governance; [Awakening leader Sheikh] Sattar referred to the Baghdad government as 'those Persians'."[141]

Instead, what appears to have been decisive in the Awakening was the popular rejection of AQI's brutality and the newfound U.S. willingness to partner directly with and empower local tribes as agents of security and governance. U.S. Army Colonel Sean MacFarland, who took over AO Topeka in the summer of 2006, lists as one of the most important lessons from his experience the realization that:

> The tribes represent the people of Iraq. . . . No matter how imperfect the tribal system appeared to us, it was capable of providing social order and control through culturally appropriate means where governmental control was weak.[142]

The often-used short hand that the United States bought off the insurgents or paid them to switch sides, therefore, is extremely misleading. No doubt some individual insurgents may have had their loyalties manipulated by money. But for the insurgency in general, U.S. payments to former insurgents cum tribal militias is more accurately described as a consequence of the change in loyalties than as a cause of the change.

In Ramadi, who governed appears to have been much more important than how those people governed.

## ENDNOTES - CHAPTER 2

1. *Baseline Food Security Analysis in Iraq,* World Food Program, September 2004, p. 78.

2. Lieutenant Colonel Justin C. Gubler and Command Sergeant Major Dennis P. Bergmann, Jr., "Task Force Rock Introduction to Ar Ramadi: Its People and the Enemy," undated briefing, p. 3.

3. Lieutenant Colonel Justin C. Gubler and Command Sergeant Major Dennis P. Bergmann, Jr., "Task Force Rock Operating Guidance," undated annotated briefing, p. 8, Interview 19 (Major Greg Sierra). All interviews will be referred to by their number and the name of the interviewee. For more detail on interview dates and interviewee positions, see Appendix I.

4. Interview 7 (Captain Sean Kuehl).

5. Interview 29 (Colonel Gary Patton).

6. Pamela Hess, "Ramadi Posts Seen As 'Symbol of Occupation'," *Washington Times*, September 7, 2004, p. 11.

7. "Introduction," *Al-Anbar Awakening, Volume I, American Perspectives: U.S. Marines and Counterinsurgency in Iraq, 2004-2009*, Chief Warrant Officer-4 Timothy S. McWilliams and Lieutenant Colonel Kurtis P. Wheeler, eds., Quantico, VA: Marine Corps University Press, 2009, p. 2.

8. Gubler and Bergmann, "Task Force Rock Operating Guidance," p. 5.

9. Interview 1 (Andrea Jackson).

10. Interview 6 (Corporal Peder Ell); Interview 23 (Carter Malkasian); Interview 36 (anonymous Army officer).

11. Seth Robson, "2nd BCT Settles Into Iraqi Home," *European Stars and Stripes*, September 11, 2004.

12. F. J. Bing West, "Iraqification, Part II," *Wall Street Journal*, August 2, 2004, p. 10.

13. 2nd Brigade Combat Team, 2nd Infantry Division, *After Action Review: Operation Iraqi Freedom 04-06, August 2004-August 2005.*

14. *Ibid.*

15. *Ibid.*

16. Hashim, p. 327.

17. Mike Dorning, "Marines Grow Weary of Even Friendly Faces," *Chicago Tribune*, September 16, 2004.

18. *Ibid.*

19. *Ibid.*

20. Anne Barnard, "US Forces, Hit By Raids, Fault Their Iraqi Allies," *Boston Globe*, August 1, 2004, p. 1; Hess, "Ramadi Posts Seen As 'Symbol of Occupation'."

21. John F. Burns and Erik Eckholm, "Western Iraq, Fundamentalists Hold U.S. at Bay," *New York Times*, August 29, 2004, p. 1.

22. "Highlights: Iraqi Press 2 Aug 04," August 2, 2004, FBIS Report GMP20040802000241, "Highlights: Iraqi Press 29 Aug 04," August 29, 2004, FBIS Report GMP20040829000187.

23. Alissa J. Rubin, "Iraqi City On Edge Of Chaos," *Los Angeles Times*, September 28, 2004, p. 1.

24. *Ibid.*

25. Seth Robson, "2nd BCT Hopes to Keep Ramadi From Turning Into Another Fallujah," *Pacific Stars and Stripes*, September 20, 2004.

26. Seth Robson, "2nd Brigade Combat Team Roundup Has Yielded 75 Suspects in Iraq," *Pacific Stars and Stripes*, October 8, 2004.

27. Interview 27 (Captain Eric Dougherty); Interview 29 (Colonel Gary Patton).

28. Joseph Giordono, "2nd Brigade Combat Team Soldiers Round Up Suspected Insurgents in Iraq," *Pacific Stars and Stripes*, October 24, 2004.

29. Edward Wong, "Provincial Capital Near Falluja Is Rapidly Slipping Into Chaos," *New York Times*, October 28, 2004, p. 1.

30. "Al Jazirah Interviews Journalist on Situation in Al-Ramadi," *Al-Jazirah Satellite Channel Television*, November 17, 2004, FBIS Report GMP20041117000050.

31. Tony Perry, "Ramadi At Heart Of Iraq Election Hopes," *Los Angeles Times*, January 22, 2005.

32. Tony Perry, "Polls Stand Empty In Sunni Stronghold," *Los Angeles Times*, January 31, 2005. One officer estimated that only 65 people voted in his battalion's area of operations, which covered approximately half the city. Interview 19 (Major Greg Sierra).

33. "IECI Head, Members in Al-Ramadi Tender Resignation," *Al-Sharqiyah*, January 28, 2005, FBIS Report GMP20050128000194.

34. Jackie Spinner, "Marines, Iraqi Forces Launch Offensive in Ramadi," *Washington Post*, February 21, 2005.

35. Joseph Giordono, "A Year On the Edge: 2nd BCT Bound for Colorado After Grueling Tour in Ramadi," *Stars and Stripes*, July 31, 2005.

36. Interview 15 (anonymous Army officer).

37. Ann Scott Tyson, "To The Dismay Of Local Sunnis, Shiites Arrive To Police Ramadi," *Washington Post*, May 7, 2005, p. 13.

38. Tom Roeder, "Carson Unit Says Tide Is Turning," *Colorado Springs Gazette*, April 18, 2005.

39. Interview 1 (Andrea Jackson).

40. Interview 3 (anonymous Army officer); Interview 36 (anonymous Army officer).

41. Interview 13 (Colonel David Clark); Interview 15 (anonymous Army officer); Interview 19 (Major Greg Sierra).

42. John Ward Anderson, "A Gruesome Find, With A Difference," *Washington Post*, March 19, 2005.

43. "U.S. Holds Secret Talks With Insurgents in Iraq," *Washington Post*, February 21, 2005; "Behind the News," *Al-Jazirah Satellite Channel Television*, June 27, 2005, FBIS Report GMP20050627535004.

44. Hamid Abdallah, "With the Americans' knowledge and consent, the Iraqi defense minister holds negotiations with the Iraqi resistance," *Al-Jazirah*, April 4, 2005, FBIS Report GMP20050404000175.

45. John A. McCary, "The Anbar Awakening: An Alliance of Incentives," *The Washington Quarterly*, Vol. 32, No. 1, January 2009, p. 48; Austin Long, "War Comes to Al Anbar: Political Conflict in an Iraqi Province," unpublished paper presented at the International Studies Association conference, February 2009, p. 11.

46. Interview 23 (Carter Malkasian); Interview 33 (Major General Richard Natonski).

47. Bing West, *The Strongest Tribe: War, Politics, and the Endgame in Iraq*, New York: Random House, 2008, p. 75.

48. *Ibid.*, p. 96.

49. Interview 32 (Lieutenant Colonel Justin Gubler); Interview 34 (Staff Sergeant Brian Fennema).

50. Nancy A. Youssef and Yasser Salihee, "Gunmen Kidnap A Governor In Iraq," *Philadelphia Inquirer*, May 11, 2005, p. 1, Ellen Knickmeyer and Othman Mohammed, "Governor In Iraq Is Found Dead," *Washington Post*, June 1, 2005, p. 16.

51. Joseph Giordono, "A Year On the Edge: 2nd BCT Bound for Colorado After Grueling Tour in Ramadi," Interview 3 (anonymous Army officer).

52. Tom Lasseter, "Insurgents Have Changed U.S. Ideas About Winning," *Philadelphia Inquirer*, August 28, 2005, p. 1.

53. Sabrina Tavernise, "Unseen Enemy Is at Its Fiercest in a Sunni City," *New York Times*, October 23, 2005, p. 1.

54. May al-Shirbini, interview with correspondent Ammar Ali, *Al-Arabiyah Television*, December 1, 2005, FBIS Report GMP20051201546007.

55. Lin Todd *et al.*, *Iraq Tribal Study – Al-Anbar Governorate*, Stockbridge, GA: Global Resources Group, June 2006, pp. 2-24.

56. Patrick Graham, "The Message From The Sunni Heartland," *New York Times*, May 22, 2005.

57. Carter Malkasian, "The Role of Perceptions and Political Reform in Counterinsurgency: The Case of Western Iraq, 2004-05," *Journal of Strategic Studies*, Vol. 17, No. 3, September 2006, pp. 371-373.

58. Hashim, pp. 71-72.

59. Christopher K. Ives, "Interview with Lieutenant Colonel John A. Nagl," from the collection *Operational Leadership Experiences in the Global War on Terrorism*, Ft. Leavenworth, KS: Combat Studies Institute, January 9, 2007.

60. Interview 32 (Lieutenant Colonel Justin Gubler).

61. Interview 19 (Major Greg Sierra).

62. Tony Perry, "U.S. General Gets Earful From Men In Sunni City Who May Forgo Polls," *Los Angeles Times*, January 30, 2005.

63. Perry, "Polls Stand Empty In Sunni Stronghold."

64. Interview 7 (Captain Sean Kuehl); a very similar comment was made in Interview 15 (anonymous Army officer).

65. "U.S. Holds Secret Talks with Insurgents in Iraq," *Washington Post*, February 21, 2005.

66. *Measuring Stability and Security in Iraq,* Washington, DC: U.S. Department of Defense, October 2005, p. 7.

67. Tyson, "To the Dismay of Local Sunnis, Shiites Arrive to Police Ramadi."

68. Interview 7 (Captain Sean Kuehl).

69. Interview 23 (Carter Malkasian); Interview 32 (Lieutenant Colonel Justin Gubler).

70. Interview 13 (Colonel David Clark).

71. Interview 3 (anonymous Army officer).

72. Interview 4 (Seth Robson).

73. Interview 6 (Corporal Peder Ell).

74. Interview 29 (Colonel Gary Patton).

75. Interview 1 (Andrea Jackson).

76. Interview 35 (Lieutenant Colonel John Fant).

77. Interview 15 (anonymous Army officer).

78. Interview 36 (anonymous Army officer).

79. Not for attribution comment from interviewee.

80. Interview 36 (anonymous Army officer).

81. Interview 13 (Colonel David Clark).

82. Interview 36 (anonymous Army officer).

83. For example, Interview 6 (Corporal Peder Ell); Interview 7 (Captain Sean Kuehl); Interview 31 (Lance Corporal Jamie Sutton).

84. Interview 29 (Colonel Gary Patton).

85. *Field Manual (FM) 3-24/Marine Corps Warfighting Publication 3-33.5, Counterinsurgency* (FM 3-24/MCWP 3-33.5), p. 1-13. The manual does also note that, "as with any fixed ratio, such calculations remain very dependent on the situation." Based on more recent analyses, even these recommended ratios may be unreliable benchmarks for successful counterinsurgency. See R. Royce Kneece Jr. *et al.*, *Force Sizing for Stability Operations*, Alexandria, VA: Institute for Defense Analyses, March 2010; and Jeffrey A. Friedman, "Manpower and Counterinsurgency: Empirical Foundations for Theory and Doctrine," *Security Studies*, Vol. 20, No. 4, 2011.

86. Interview 27 (Captain Eric Dougherty). For a broader treatment of this subject see Carter Malkasian, "Did the U.S. Need More Forces in Iraq? Evidence from Al Anbar," *Joint Force Quarterly*, Issue 46, 3rd Quarter 2007, pp. 120-126.

87. Interview 29 (Colonel Gary Patton).

88. Interview 13 (Colonel David Clark).

89. Interview 3 (anonymous Army officer).

90. West, *The Strongest Tribe*, p. 71.

91. Interview 5 (Captain Ed Rapisarda).

92. Interview 32 (Lieutenant Colonel Justin Gubler); Interview 36 (anonymous Army officer).

93. Interview 4 (Seth Robson); Interview 6 (Corporal Peder Ell); Interview 27 (Captain Eric Dougherty); Sheikh Ahmad Bezia Fteikhan al-Rishawi; Interview 3 (anonymous Army officer); Colonel Gary W. Montgomery and Chief Warrant Officer-4 Timothy S. McWilliams, eds., *Al-Anbar Awakening, Volume II, Iraqi Perspectives: From Insurgency to Counterinsurgency in Iraq, 2004-2009*, Quantico, VA: Marine Corps University Press, 2009, p. 50.

94. John Hendren, "U.S. Troops Still Dying In Ramadi Amid 'Relative Peace, Tranquility,'" *Los Angeles Times*, December 1, 2004; Interview 35 (Lieutenant Colonel John Fant).

95. "US Military Says 'Insurgents' Blew Up Red Crescent Offices in Al-Ramadi," *Agent France Press*, October 8, 2004, FBIS Report EUP20041008000429.

96. Interview 13 (Colonel David Clark).

97. Interview 7 (Captain Sean Kuehl).

98. Interview 35 (Lieutenant Colonel John Fant).

99. Giordono, "2nd Brigade Combat Team Soldiers Round Up Suspected Insurgents in Iraq."

100. Rubin, "Iraqi City On Edge Of Chaos."

101. Interview 5 (Captain Ed Rapisarda).

102. *Rebuilding Iraq: Resource, Security, Governance, Essential Services, and Oversight Issues*, GAO-04-902R, Washington, DC: U.S. General Accounting Office, June 2004, p. 90.

103. *Measuring Stability and Security in Iraq*, Washington, DC: U.S. Department of Defense, May 2006, p. 25.

104. Iraqi Reconstruction Management System, U.S. Army Corps of Engineers, Gulf Region Division, June 2008. Available data on CERP spending totals include total funds distributed and project start dates and end dates. The author has estimated monthly and quarterly spending totals based on equal division of total funds spent over the number of active months per project. Project lengths in the database range from 1 to 40 months, but the average length is 4 months. As a result, aggregate quarterly spending summaries (as reported in the text above) are less likely to be distorted by this estimation technique than the monthly spending estimates (as shown in the figure).

105. Dana Hedgpeth and Sarah Cohen, "Money as a Weapon," *Washington Post*, August 11, 2008 (see both article and the transcript of the online discussion: *www.washingtonpost.com/wp-dyn/content/discussion/2008/08/10/DI2008081001774.html?sid=ST2008081002653&s_pos=list*).

106. Dana Hedgpeth and Sarah Cohen, "In Ramadi, a Counterinsurgency in Cash," *Washington Post*, August 11, 2008.

107. Eli Berman, Jacob N. Shapiro, and Joseph H Felter, "Can Hearts and Minds Be Bought? The Economics of Counterinsurgency in Iraq," *Journal of Political Economy*, Vol. 119, No. 4, August 2011.

108. Hedgpeth and Cohen, "In Ramadi, a Counterinsurgency in Cash."

109. Hedgpeth and Cohen, "Money as a Weapon."

110. Interview 13 (Colonel David Clark); Interview 32 (Lieutenant Colonel Justin Gubler).

111. Interview 29 (Colonel Gary Patton).

112. Wong, "Provincial Capital Near Falluja Is Rapidly Slipping Into Chaos."

113. "Al-Ramadi Residents Begin 2-day Sit-in in Protest of US Forces' Practices," *Al-Sharqiyah Television*, May 7, 2005, FBIS Report GMP20050507542005.

114. West, *The Strongest Tribe*, p. 24.

115. Joe Klein, "Saddam's Revenge," *Time*, September 18, 2005.

116. Interview 13 (Colonel David Clark).

117. West, *The Strongest Tribe*, p. 96.

118. Interview 33 (Major General Richard Natonski).

119. Malkasian,"The Role of Perceptions and Political Reform in Counterinsurgency: The Case of Western Iraq, 2004-05," pp. 373-374.

120. Lieutenant Colonel Justin C. Gubler, "Reconciling Counterinsurgency with Civil War: A Strategy for Stabilizing Iraq," unpublished paper, March 26, 2007, p. 7.

121. Interview 5 (Captain Ed Rapisarda).

122. Interview 26 (Tony Perry).

123. Interview 29 (Colonel Gary Patton).

124. Interview 32 (Lieutenant Colonel Justin Gubler).

125. Interview 19 (Major Greg Sierra).

126. Interview 23 (Carter Malkasian).

127. Interview 15 (anonymous Army officer).

128. Interview 29 (Colonel Gary Patton).

129. Interview 19 (Major Greg Sierra); Interview 29 (Colonel Gary Patton); Interview 32 (Lieutenant Colonel Justin Gubler).

130. Interview 19 (Major Greg Sierra).

131. Gubler and Bergmann, "Task Force Rock Introduction to Ar Ramadi: Its People and the Enemy," p. 41. (RPG=Rocket Propelled Grenade, RPK=assault rifle, PKM=machine gun, ISF=Iraqi Security Forces, IP=Iraqi Police, IED=Improvised Explosive Device, SVBIED=Suicide Vehicle-Borne IED, MSR=Main Supply Route, BLACK=unsafe, CF=Coalition Forces.)

132. 2nd Brigade Combat Team, 2nd Infantry Division, *After Action Review: Operation Iraqi Freedom 04-06, August 2004 – August 2005*.

133. Interview 19 (Major Greg Sierra).

134. Interview 35 (Lieutenant Colonel John Fant).

135. Statement of David M. Walker before the Subcommittee on National Security, Emerging Threats, and International Relations, Committee on Government Reform, House of Representatives, *Rebuilding Iraq: Governance, Security, Reconstruction, and Financing Challenges*, GAO-06-697T, Washington, DC: U.S. Government Accountability Office, April 25, 2006, p. 11.

136. For one expression of such concern, see Austin Long, "The Anbar Awakening," *Survival*, Vol. 50, No. 2, April-May 2008, pp. 67-68, 83.

137. *Measuring Stability and Security in Iraq,* Washington, DC: U.S. Department of Defense, February 2006, pp. 24-25.

138. Oliver Poole, "Insurgents Turning Against Al-Qa'ida in Iraq," *The Daily Telegraph*, February 6, 2006.

139. David Kilcullen, "Religion and Insurgency," *Small Wars Journal Blog*, May 12, 2007.

140. See Major Niel Smith and Colonel Sean MacFarland, "Anbar Awakens: The Tipping Point," *Military Review*, March-April 2008, pp. 41-52; Long (2008); Long (2009); McCary.

141. Bing West, "Counterinsurgency Lessons From Iraq," *Military Review*, March-April 2009, pp. 10-11.

142. Smith and MacFarland, p. 52.

# CHAPTER 3

## TAL AFAR (MAY 2005 to FEBRUARY 2006)

This chapter presents a case study of U.S. operations in and around the city of Tal Afar from May 2005 to February 2006. Its focus is on the U.S. Army's 3rd Armored Cavalry Regiment (3ACR) and its subordinate units during that time period. Like the case in Chapter 2, this case is presented in seven parts covering the following topics: 1) an overview of the background and major events of the case; 2) the role of ethnic and religious identity politics in the case; 3) counterinsurgent actions with respect to providing security; 4) counterinsurgent actions with respect to improving governance; 5) any efforts toward political agreements that address ethno-religious cleavages; 6) an assessment of the outcome of the counterinsurgency; and 7) a concluding discussion and evaluation of the case in the context of this study's questions and analytic framework.

## CASE BACKGROUND

### Tal Afar and the Insurgency.

The commander of the U.S. Army's 3rd Armored Cavalry Regiment, Colonel H. R. McMaster, commented that "If you take all the complexities of Iraq and compressed [sic] it into one city, it is Tal Afar."[1] Tal Afar is a small city in Iraq's northern Ninewah province. It is located roughly equidistant (50-60 miles) between Ninewah's capital city of Mosul to the east and the Syrian border to the west. Though population estimates for Tal Afar are as high as 300,000,[2] most estimates are closer to 200,000, and some interviewees were convinced that the city's population by 2005 was much lower, perhaps only 100,000 people or fewer.[3] Tal Afar's population is distinct for being less than 10 percent Arab; 90 percent of the population is ethnic Turkmen. Tal Afar's Turkmen are Muslims, but split between about 75 percent Sunni and 25 percent Shi'a.

In spite of its somewhat remote and isolated position, Tal Afar has been a strategically important city throughout Iraq's history, including during the most recent war. Like Ramadi, it has served as something of a gateway for travelers, merchants, and smugglers, as well as being a pathway for oil pipelines transiting in and out of Iraq. It also straddles the boundary among Turkish, Kurdish, and Arab ethnic communities and bears the imprint of each of those rival groups. Though predominantly Turkmen, it had a heavily Arab culture during Saddam Hussein's rule, and its strategic location is coveted by the nearby Kurds.[4] (See Figure 3-1.)

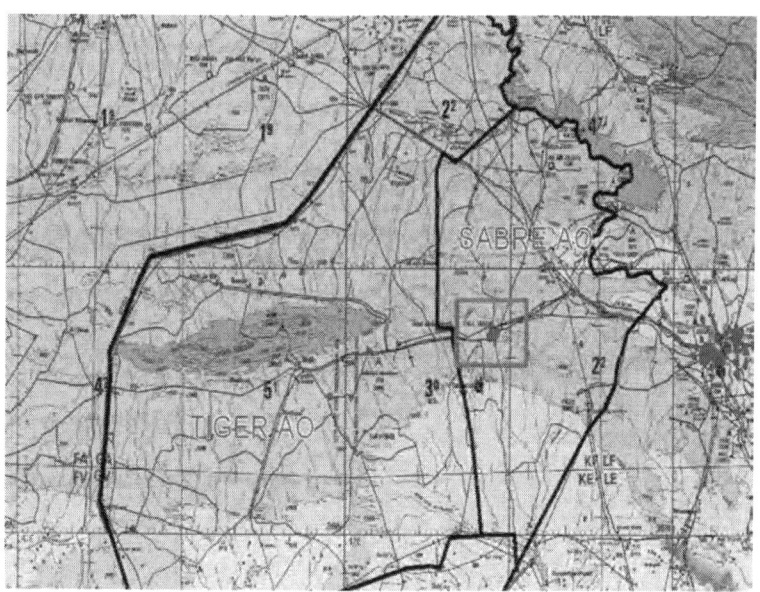

**Figure 3-1. Tal Afar and Western Ninewah Province.[5]**

In recent decades, Tal Afar's economy was primarily based on four sectors: agriculture, trucking, smuggling, and government.[6] This latter sector became particularly important in the aftermath of the U.S. invasion. Many of Tal Afar's Turkmen were very loyal Ba'athists and had been strong supporters of Saddam Hussein. And, again like Ramadi, many current and former soldiers of Iraq's Army resided in Tal Afar, creating a solid basis for technical and tactical expertise in organizing armed opposition to the new forces in power.[7] Tal Afar was disproportionately represented in Saddam Hussein's secret police, so much so that the idiomatic expression, "watch out for him, he's from Tal Afar," meant he was a person with connections to Saddam Hussein's ruthless internal security institutions.[8]

Partly as a result of these relationships, and partly because of its location, the city fairly quickly became a focal point of insurgent activity in 2003-04. It was both a strategic transit point for foreign insurgents entering Iraq, and a home to many local Sunnis who were strongly opposed to the U.S. presence and the installation of a new government in Baghdad that was friendly with Iran and that equated Ba'athists with terrorists. As in Ramadi, this common cause became the basis for an early alliance between Islamic radicals and more secular Iraqis opposed to the new order. In the summer of 2004, this alliance of insurgents routed the local police force and all but took control of the city.[9] One report referred to the city at the time as a "guerrilla bastion where the U.S.-backed interim Iraqi government exerts only limited control."[10]

In September 2004, the U.S.-led Coalition initiated a major offensive against Tal Afar, known as Operation BLACK TYPHOON, in an attempt to dislodge the insurgents from their stronghold in the city. Coalition forces conducted what amounted to a siege of the city for 2 weeks. Then on September 12, two U.S. battalions and an Iraqi National Guard battalion moved into the city in a major assault. As it turned out, they encountered little resistance from insurgents, as most had apparently fled.[11]

American officials at the time were not committed to conducting a counterinsurgency in the city. Instead, in keeping with the Coalition's larger strategy of transition, as well as with the economy of force levels of resources available, they wanted to get out of the city quickly. The senior U.S. officer in the area, Brigadier General Carter Ham, said:

> Having us stay there is exactly the wrong thing. First of all, we don't have enough forces to stay in the city. But it also sends a message to those that oppose us. It lets them say, 'See, we told you, they really are occupiers. They've taken over a city.'[12]

The aftermath of Operation BLACK TYPHOON was very difficult for the people of Tal Afar. Essential services were nonfunctional, and many of the city's residents were denied the freedom to return to their homes. Half or more of the city's residents were temporarily displaced. The resulting humanitarian problems generated grave protests against the United States from the Turkish government.[13] Insurgents fairly quickly reasserted their freedom of action and control in the city.

The Army unit that took over responsibility for Tal Afar in the spring of 2005 divided the insurgency there into two groups, borrowing locally-used terms that echoed the threat assessment in Ramadi: "Resistance" and "Takfiri." According to that unit's reports:

The 'Resistance' was made up of primarily Sunni Turkoman, supported by internal and external Islamic Extremist elements, whose fundamental goal was to prevent the Iraqi Transitional Government from succeeding, stall the growing power of the Shia local leaders throughout the AO [Area of Operations], and prevent the re-establishment of security forces which were not representative of the Sunni Turkoman population or its long term desires. The 'Takfiri' consisted of Islamic Extremist elements . . . [that] sought to end the occupation of the area by Coalition Forces, force the failure of the Iraqi Transitional Government (ITG), and establish a Muslim Rule of Law based largely upon the ideology adopted by Al-Qaida and the Taliban in Afghanistan.[14]

As in Anbar, these two groups were somewhat distinct but operated in concert against their common enemies, the Coalition and the Iraqi government.

The "Takfiri" elements within the insurgency in Tal Afar received a great deal of attention, partly due to the U.S. Government's public emphasis on fighting al-Qaeda, and partly due to their truly grisly acts of terrorism in the city, which featured suicide bombings and leaving beheaded bodies lying in the streets. Colonel McMaster described the enemy in Tal Afar as "the worst of the worst . . . people in the world."[15] Nevertheless, the available evidence, including the interviews conducted for this research, shows that most of the insurgents in the city were local Sunni Turkmen, not foreigners.[16] For example, one cavalry troop detained over 350 people during the course of its time in the city, 90-95 percent of whom were local Sunni Turkmen.[17] As the regiment's operations officer, Major Michael Simmering, indicated:

Everyone talks about Tal Afar being an important logistical hub for the foreign fighters coming into the country from Syria, but we didn't really see a lot of that. . . . [C]ertainly AQI was present and definitely fed the fire, but the insurgency was primarily locally-funded, locally-led, locally-focused.[18]

## The Counterinsurgents.

Like the 2nd Brigade Combat Team, 2nd Infantry Division (2/2ID) in Ramadi, 3ACR operated under a divisional headquarters (known at the time as Multi-National Forces–Northwest) and a corps headquarters (Multi-National Corps-Iraq [MNC-I]) in Baghdad. 3ACR, a unit slightly larger than, but roughly equivalent to, a brigade combat team, was composed of five squadrons, each the rough equivalent of a battalion: three cavalry squadrons, one aviation squadron, and one support squadron. The design and training of a cavalry regiment features elements potentially both advantageous and disadvantageous to conducting counterinsurgency operations. In conventional, high-intensity armored warfare, the role of cavalry units is primarily as scouts, performing reconnaissance and screening missions in support of larger armored formations. These missions put a premium on both mobility and collection and processing of intelligence. The former requirement means that cavalry units tend to be very dependent on the armored vehicles around which their units are built. This tactical culture is perhaps an obstacle to adapting to counterinsurgency operations that involve foot patrols and extensive interaction with the local population. On the other hand, the focus and force structure that a cavalry unit normally dedicates to intelligence does provide a solid foundation for adapting to counterinsurgency, a traditionally intelligence-driven mission.

3ACR was originally designated to operate in an area just outside Baghdad, but as U.S. commanders grew more concerned about Tal Afar's deterioration, four of its five squadrons were reassigned to western Ninewah province shortly after arriving in Iraq. First Squadron ("Tiger Squadron") moved into the expansive Syrian border area and western desert, while Second Squadron ("Sabre Squadron") took responsibility for Tal Afar, itself. The aviation and support squadrons also moved with Tiger and Sabre. The regiment's units began arriving in Ninewah in April, with about 4,000 troops having settled in by the middle of May. Sabre Squadron, with around 1,300 troops, officially assumed responsibility for the city of Tal Afar on May 1, 2005. 3ACR transferred authority to its successor on February 19, 2006.[19]

### What Happened (May 2005 to February 2006).

In the months after Operation BLACK TYPHOON, western Ninewah province had received only the thinnest coverage by U.S. forces. When 3ACR took control of the area, it approximately quadrupled the number of troops in the area of operations. With so few forces in the area, the United States and the still very weak Iraqi security forces had not been able to resist a gradual takeover of Tal Afar by insurgents. Soldiers described the city as a ghost town[20] where economic activity had all but ceased,[21] families feared leaving their homes, and U.S. forces were attacked every time they ventured out from their bases.[22] A Sabre Squadron platoon leader reported that "the first 3 months were essentially an extended armed reconnaissance."[23]

The city's neighborhoods had become tribal and sectarian enclaves where, for example, Sunni Farhats rarely ventured into Shi'a Jolaq areas and vice versa.[24] Tal Afar's mayor, a Sunni, was widely known to be working with the insurgents. The police force, meanwhile, or at least what remained of it, was entirely Shi'a. Described by some interviewees as little more than a sectarian death squad,[25] the police tended to stay holed up at the city's Ottoman-era hilltop castle in a Shi'a neighborhood, only venturing out to conduct attacks on rival tribal groups.

3ACR's first moves were to try to clear some key locations in the city, such as around the hospital, to secure the main east-west highway and to attempt to start reconstituting the police force. After initial unsuccessful attacks against the U.S. forces, insurgents began targeting civilians more. One local tribal leader complained, "Anyone not helping the terrorists can't leave their homes because they will be kidnapped and the terrorists will demand money or weapons or make them join them to kill people. If they refuse they will chop their heads off." A flier posted at a school read, "If you love your children, you won't send them to school here because we will kill them."[26] This trend was punctuated by a pivotal attack on May 23 when Sunni insurgents detonated two large suicide car bombs in the neighborhood of the Jolaq tribe, one of the city's largest Shi'a tribes, killing or injuring more than 40 people. Sabre Squadron commander Lieutenant Colonel Chris Hickey called this incident a turning point for the Jolaq tribe, who turned to the United States for help and "created the opening needed to allow our Soldiers and leaders to finally begin understanding the city."[27]

On June 4, in what was to be the beginning of one of Sabre Squadron's main efforts in Tal Afar, Hickey hosted a summit of tribal sheikhs to discuss how to solve the security situation in the city. More than 60 local leaders attended, and to the Americans' surprise, amid a great deal of tension, argument, and raised voices, many of the sheikhs in attendance advocated a major military assault on the city.[28] In large part, however, this reflected a deep sectarian split among Tal Afar's tribes. Shi'a tribal leaders were much readier for a military solution than were Sunni tribal leaders, and they each lobbied the provincial and federal governments to this effect.[29] The minority Shi'a saw the United States as a potential ally in protecting them from their Sunni rivals and were quite ready to paint those groups with a broad insurgent brush. As one Sabre trooper put it, "These guys weren't interested in fighting insurgency. They were interested in using an armored cavalry regiment to carry out their tribal vendettas."[30]

For the first half of the blazing hot summer, 3ACR resisted entreaties for a major assault on the city, continuing to try to identify and target known insurgents while trying to build relationships with the complex network of competing sheikhs in the city. In spite of tactical successes, however, the city remained gripped by fear and violence. By late July, the regiment had decided that a major offensive would be necessary to clear some parts of the city of the worst of the insurgents there. Thus began an elaborate, multiweek preparation for an attack focused on Tal Afar's eastern Sarai neighborhood, an attack that would be known as Operation RESTORING RIGHTS.

Key features of these preparations included marshalling several Iraqi Army and police commando units, together with their U.S. Special Forces advisors, building a dirt berm around the city to limit movement in and out of the city, and constructing a large facility outside the city for residents to take shelter away from the combat.[31] The regiment also brought more than half of Tiger Squadron into the western half of the city from its posts in the desert and along the border, and arranged for a battalion of the 82nd Airborne Division (2nd Battalion, 325th Airborne Infantry Regiment [2-325th]) to move into the targeted Sarai neighborhood immediately following the assault.

In some respects, these preparations and the plans for the operation, itself, bore the hallmarks of a very conventional combat operation. Its intent, however, aligned with the regiment's understanding of the political dynamics in the city, as Lieutenant Colonel Hickey explains:

> The overarching purpose of Operation RESTORING RIGHTS (ORR) was to set the conditions in which political and economic development could proceed. More specifically, by attacking the Takfirists and guarding against the tendency to attack the population directly, the Sunni could be reintegrated into the mainstream political process once the veil of terror was lifted from their ranks. Meanwhile, maintaining the support of the Shiites could eventually bring unity to the city and establish an environment that finally allowed for reconstruction operations and reconciliation of tribal conflicts.[32]

With this objective in mind, U.S. and Iraqi security forces kicked off the operation on September 2. For nearly 2 weeks, U.S. and Iraqi forces cordoned off and then moved through the Sarai district and other eastern portions of the city, facilitating civilian evacuation, targeting known insurgent strongholds, and clearing city blocks. Resistance to the assault force was much lighter than anticipated, in part because of the Iraqi government's insistence on a 7-day pause for civilian evacuation, which some believe allowed many insurgents to escape.[33]

By September 15, the operation had concluded, with U.S. and Iraqi forces having killed around 150 insurgents and captured another 850.[34] Crucially, U.S. forces opted to remain stationed inside the city for the first time, with the newly arrived 2-325th battalion taking over the Sarai neighborhood and Sabre Squadron taking up headquarters in the northern and central areas of the city. This began a period of major reconstruction and political activism on the part of 3ACR. In October, Sabre Squadron established the following goals for its operations in the city:[35]

- Quickly establish security forces throughout the depth of the city to secure the population prior to the return of the majority of the civilians.
- Establish [traffic control points] and obstacles throughout the city to control the ability of the [anti-Iraqi forces] to maneuver freely throughout the city.
- Recruit, train, equip, and employ a police force representative of the population.
- Immediately address any claims of damages made by the citizens and pay compensation.
- Begin large scale reconstruction operations to immediately begin altering perceptions of security.
- Target anti-Iraqi forces operating within the city to prevent them from reinitiating their campaign of intimidation on the population.
- Immediately establish new operational police stations throughout the city to begin the process of transitioning security responsibilities to local forces.

- Conduct information operations to emphasize the legitimacy of the government, the necessity of ORR [Operation RESTORING RIGHTS], and the return of peace and security to Tal Afar.
- Ensure each citizen of Tal Afar [is] afforded the opportunity to vote in the October Referendum.

Three of these goals stood out in importance. First was the establishment of new security stations throughout the city, jointly manned by U.S. and Iraqi forces. The idea behind this initiative was to establish a ubiquitous presence in the city and thus raise the confidence of the population while expanding intelligence collection and limiting insurgents' freedom of movement.

Second was the recruitment of a new police force. In particular, U.S. forces aimed to create a police force that was representative of the sectarian demographics of the city, as opposed to being dominated by the Shi'a minority as had been the case previously. As Lieutenant Colonel Hickey explained:

> Prior to ORR [Operation RESTORING RIGHTS], Sabre attempted to recruit police from throughout the city. Because of the enemy's campaign of intimidation, Sunni citizens did not volunteer in significant numbers. The police recruiting process began upon the completion of ORR and became an immediate success. In the first 2 days of police recruiting, over 300 people arrived at the castle to volunteer to become [Iraqi police]; the more important part of the number was that 60-70% of the people that arrived were Sunni.[36]

Third was the preparation for the fall elections, the constitutional referendum in October and national elections in December. Substantial popular participation in these elections was seen as a critical measure of political development in the fledgling state. Sabre Squadron counted the elections as a significant success in Tal Afar. There were no major attacks and an estimated 17,000 people voted in October, and 40,000 in December, a great improvement over 1,000 estimated voters in the January 2005 election.[37]

These efforts accompanied a significant push to reestablish the basic functioning of the city's infrastructure and services, especially provision of clean water and food. And 3ACR commanders continued their attempts to bring Tal Afar's tribal sheikhs into a political process that might eventually form the foundation for a new city government.

Violence in Tal Afar plummeted over the fall of 2005. Figure 3-2 shows the average number of daily attacks in each of the 10 months from April 2005 to January 2006.[38] These numbers include attacks by multiple methods against U.S. forces, Iraqi security forces, as well as civilian targets in the city. Attacks declined over this period from an average of six per day in June 2005 to about one per day in December. At the end of that month, the 2-385th battalion left the city, leaving Sabre Squadron as the main U.S. unit in the city. Nevertheless, violence continued its decline into January, when Tal Afar experienced only 18 insurgent attacks all month.

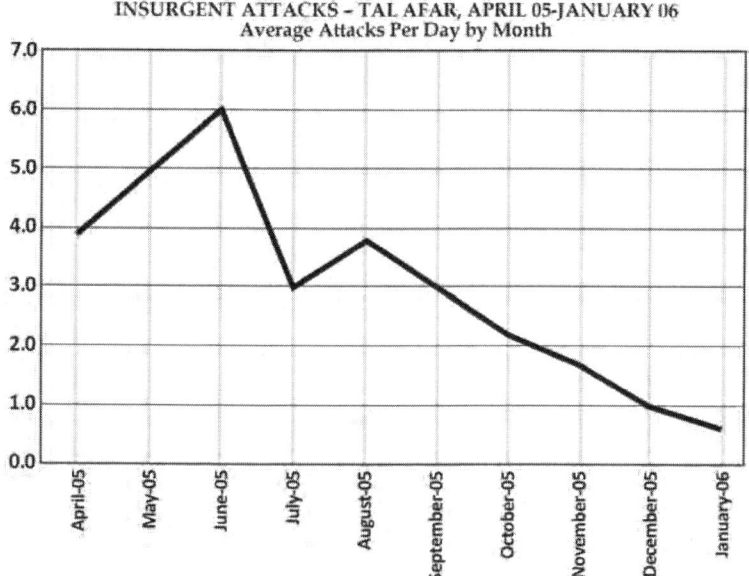

Figure 3-2. Average Attacks Per Day in Tal Afar.

In February 2006, shortly before 3ACR turned Tal Afar over to its successors, the 1st Brigade of the 1st Armored Division, the city's sheikhs held a tribal reconciliation meeting. Leading sheikhs from both Sunni and Shi'a tribes held civil discussions about the future administration of the city and proclaimed themselves to be not just Sunni or Shi'a, but "Iraqian."[39]

In the months after 3ACR's departure, Tal Afar was not free from insurgent activity or from sectarian violence. Some of the same tensions that had plagued the city before persisted,[40] not least because of the sectarian violence that swept much of Iraq in the wake of the bombing of the al Askariya Mosque in Samarra, only 3 days after 3ACR left Ninewah. But the city did not regress back into the ungovernable war zone that it had been.

The transformation of Tal Afar from insurgent stronghold to a moderately functional city quickly became a touchstone for policymakers in conceiving of a shift in U.S. strategy in Iraq toward the concept deemed to have been practiced there: "clear, hold, and build." In October 2005 Senate testimony, Secretary of State Condoleeza Rice cited Tal Afar as a successful example of this approach.[41] President George W. Bush dedicated an entire speech to 3ACR's experiences in Tal Afar as an illustration of what was possible for the United States to achieve in Iraq.[42] Subsequently, it featured in the Army's and Marine Corps's new counterinsurgency manual, again as a successful example of "clear, hold, and build."[43]

## Were Ethno-Religious Identity-Based Cleavages Significant?

There is no question that Sunni-Shi'a identity-based conflict was central to the insurgency in Tal Afar. The conflict was manifest in two mutually reinforcing dimensions: the national conflict between Sunnis who were increasingly afraid of disenfranchisement at the hands of the allegedly sectarian central government; and local conflict among tribes who were predominantly Sunni or Shi'a.

This sectarian cleavage is something of a historical curiosity because it had not been a significant problem among Tal Afar's Turkmen population prior to the overthrow of Saddam Hussein.[44] To the contrary, Tal Afar's Sunni and Shi'a were united to some degree by pride in the distinctness of their Turkmen culture and language in a majority-Arab country. But in the aftermath of the Coalition invasion of Iraq, the Turkmen were experiencing what one scholar called an identity crisis.[45] Their political mobilization had been almost entirely based in the Ba'ath party, which was now not

91

only out of power but illegal, a problem one interviewee likened to "pulling the spinal column out of Iraq."[46] What would replace Ba'athism was uncertain, but to the extent Tal Afar's Sunnis could discern the intentions of the new Iraqi government, they feared sectarian discrimination. One interviewee characterized the views of the Sunni Turkmen elite as nationalist, but with "almost a colonial mentality; 'our Shi'a' are OK, we can handle them. But the 'other Shi'a', they are compromised, they have come under the sway of the Iranians."[47]

Additionally, with the collapse of the state that had provided virtually everything to the city, from security to food, the people of Tal Afar increasingly looked to their tribes for sources of support. While Tal Afar's tribes do not share an entirely homogeneous religion, they do tend to be predominantly Sunni or Shi'a.[48] Soon these emerging tribal — and increasingly sectarian — grievances were being stoked by the Islamist extremists who were taking up residence in the city in growing numbers, thanks in part to its strategic location as a transit point between Syria and Mosul and then Baghdad. This was the environment that became fertile ground for an alliance of convenience between nationalist local resistance insurgents and the Islamist radicals of al-Qaeda in Iraq (AQI) and Ansar al Sunna. Very quickly, then, the city descended into a nightmare of tribal feuds and terror imposed by the insurgents. In this sense, as one interviewee put it, the conflict in Tal Afar was "sectarian-fueled" but not "sectarian-based."[49]

The sectarian cleavage was further exacerbated by the behavior of many of the Iraqi security forces that operated in and around the city. The police were taken over by a Shi'a chief who quickly purged the leading Sunni officers from the force, prompting rumors of the growing local influence of the Iranian-backed Badr Corps militia.[50] The Iraqi Army also tended to reinforce the fears the Sunnis had of being marginalized, or worse. In Operation BLACK TYPHOON, the Army's Scorpion Brigade, a heavily Shi'a commando unit, was deployed to Tal Afar from Baghdad, inciting loud protests from Tal Afar's Sunnis. Voicing a common complaint, one resident complained that all the official security forces "are from the Badr Organization and the [Kurdish] Pesh Merga. They wear the military uniform for disguise. Their treatment is very bad. They were taking people to detention prisons just because they are Sunnis since the start of the military campaign." Another resident agreed, saying: "The Iraqi army are the real terrorists. Even what they write on our walls is evidence, like 'Long live Pesh Merga' or 'Long live Badr.'"[51] Just as Tal Afar's Sunnis had begun to see Badr behind every Shi'a, Shi'a were quick to label any Sunni as a terrorist.[52]

Another measure of the division and animosity that had developed in the city was the reaction of Sunnis in the Sarai district when told that they needed to evacuate through a Shi'a neighborhood. The majority of them refused to do so, having been warned that Shi'a residents and police in that neighborhood would attack them if they left in that direction. One man explained, "I would rather die from American bombs in my home with my family than walk south. People are saying the Shiites will kill you or kidnap you." Another resident of the Sarai neighborhood commented: "There are no bad people in Sarai. If you come with me, I will take you to all the houses and you can see. The bad people are the Shiites in the south [of the city]."[53]

Tal Afar's appearance as something of a micro-cosm of a brewing civil war was not lost on Iraqi leaders in Baghdad. As Operation RESTORING RIGHTS went forward in September 2005, debates raged over it in Baghdad, with Sunni and Shi'a politicians leveling accusations of sectarianism with equal gusto. Shi'a politicians cast the operations as a legitimate government intervention aimed at ceasing Sunni oppression of the city's Shi'a minority. For example Ali Al-Dabbagh claimed that "we support [what the government is doing] 100 percent. Tal Afar has been a bleeding wound in Iraq's heart for a year now. There was a clear case of racial and ethnic cleansing in the city." Others contended that the conflict was not originally a sectarian one, but that the government response was making it one. Sunni lawmaker Salih al-Mutlaq, for example, said, "The tension is between the people and the government, not between the Sunnis and Shiites. [In Tal Afar, the government is waging] a very ugly ethnic war."[54] Another Sunni politician, Fakhri al-Qaysi, argued that accusations of terrorism were only a pretext for marginalizing the political participation of Sunni communities. "The ruling political parties and the U.S. forces are trying to provoke the Sunni Arabs . . . and press to harp on the tune of sectarianism as they have been doing since the first day of occupation."[55]

## Were Good Security Operations Conducted?

A description of security operations in Tal Afar usefully divide into the periods before and after Operation RESTORING RIGHTS. Before the operation, U.S. forces mostly lived on forward operating bases outside the city and would move into and around the city in their armored vehicles. Dismounted patrols were conducted regularly as well, but the commute to work was an important feature of operations. Frequently, operations took on the character of movement to contact, where the patrol's agenda would be set by responding to enemy engagements.

3ACR forces also conducted a good deal of targeted operations — raids and strikes — against insurgent suspects or facilities. However, the quality of the intelligence it used for targeting was significantly hampered by two closely related factors. First, because of their sporadic presence in the city, they had to rely on informants to generate much of what intelligence could not be gathered electronically. But in the regiment's first couple months in the area, members of Shi'a tribes were the only local residents willing to work with the U.S. forces. Over time, 3ACR learned that many of these allies were not only unreliable, but counterproductive. Interviewees report incidents where informants had identified individuals, or even just groupings of houses tied to the insurgency, when in fact, they were simply pursuing tribal rivals.[56] As a result, until U.S. forces recognized that they were being manipulated, they "actually exacerbated the problem to some extent, by rolling up Sunnis, not all of whom were bad guys," said Major Simmering.[57] One troop commander lamented that "our increased cooperation with the Shi'a tribes confirmed the Sunni population's worst fears."[58] Another said simply, "up until Operation RESTORING RIGHTS, we were pretty much fighting a losing battle."[59]

After Operation RESTORING RIGHTS, however, the situation changed dramatically. Many factors changed in that period, including some of those described in the next two sections. But one of the most important initiatives of this time was the movement of

95

U.S. forces (specifically Sabre Squadron and 2-325th) into the city and into small, neighborhood outposts that were jointly manned by U.S. and Iraqi forces.

It was only at this point that U.S. forces were really able to start providing a strong, constant presence, which in turn allowed them to develop the relationships with the people that generated good intelligence. Troop commanders reported that staying in the city was a tough sell to their troops at first, but that the visible changes their presence brought were eventually very good for morale.[60] More patrolling occurred, both by U.S. and Iraqi forces, at section and squad level rather than platoon level, because the improved security environment allowed it. As a result, Lieutenant Colonel Hickey said, "the perception of the amount of coalition forces operating within the city changed significantly as more and more units became visible to the populace on a daily basis."[61]

U.S. security operations in Tal Afar were also aided significantly by the availability and generally good performance of Iraqi security forces. Through most of its tenure in Ninewah, 3ACR partnered with the 1st Brigade of the 3rd Iraqi Army Division. The brigade was predominantly Kurdish and Shi'a, which did sometimes generate friction with Tal Afar's Sunni majority, as noted above. However, the unit received praise from many interviewees for its skill, professionalism, and leadership, especially the commander of the 3rd Iraqi Army Division, Major General Khorsheed Saleem al-Dosekey.[62] In Colonel McMaster's judgment, "the most important aspect of building local legitimacy was the legitimacy of the [Iraqi security forces]."[63]

Another key factor in security operations was the sheer number of forces that the Coalition was able to bring to bear on the fight for Tal Afar. Precise counts are difficult, and the forces focused on the city varied considerably over time. But by virtually any measure, the military presence in Tal Afar was quite large relative to the size of the city and its population. At its peak during Operation RESTORING RIGHTS, the force presence in the city included 2,000-4,000 U.S. troops and 3,000-6,000 Iraqi troops, including Army, police, and commando units. As noted, population estimates for this time also vary greatly, but even the most conservative estimate of the force-to-population ratio would be 1:40, and it could have gone as high as 1:10.[64] Anywhere in this range would qualify as a relatively high troop density, especially considering that the city of Tal Afar only covers approximately nine square kilometers. Interestingly, McMaster initially wanted even more troops for the assault.[65] His judgment on the importance of troop density was that success "could have been possible with a smaller number of troops, but it would have taken a lot longer."[66] Of course, fewer forces were present for most of the period of the case study, but during the critical months of September to December, both Sabre Squadron and 2-325th Battalion, as well as large portions of the Iraqi Army's 1st Brigade, 3rd Division exclusively focused on the city.

The combination of troop density and persistent presence throughout the city clearly played a major role in reducing the violence in Tal Afar and setting the city back on a path toward a semblance of normalcy. On balance, this record suggests that good security operations were conducted in Tal Afar.

## Was Good Governance Provided?

As with security operations, the 3ACR's efforts to improve governance in Tal Afar were quite different before and after Operation RESTORING RIGHTS. When the regiment arrived, Tal Afar's city government was all but abandoned, and basic services had drastically deteriorated. Responsibility for taking care of the city's people had largely devolved to the city's many tribal leaders,[67] but economic activity had largely ceased, creating an epidemic of unemployment for many of those who did not leave the city. In some cases, infrastructure failures fell disproportionately on the Shi'a tribes. One prominent grievance was the collection of the raw sewage that drained into a wooded area next to one of the city's mainly Shi'a neighborhoods — a site that 3ACR Soldiers dubbed the "Shitwood Forest."

Echoing 2/2ID's experience in Ramadi, most of 3ACR's efforts to re-establish good governance in its first few months in the city were frustrated by the persistent violence and the absence of many reliable Iraqi partners willing to work with them. First Lieutenant Brian Tinklepaugh described an example of the difficulties facing projects aimed to improve governance during this time. His troop established a program to deliver water in trucks to a predominantly Sunni neighborhood that was suffering from unreliable water pressure and electricity. They hired Sunni truck drivers and sent along police to provide security for the trucks. The Shi'a police soon told the U.S. Soldiers that they were hiring insurgents. When the United States then arrested the truck drivers, they alienated those drivers' tribes, whose leadership stopped supporting the Coalition's reconstruction operations.[68]

Rebuilding the city and reestablishing the basic functions of governance beyond security were central to the planning behind Operation RESTORING RIGHTS. Lieutenant Colonel Hickey called reconstruction the most important phase of the operation. He explains:

> Regardless of how many people Sabre captured or killed, if the people didn't feel secure, essential services were not re-established, and viable alternatives to engaging in terrorist activities were not made available, Tal Afar would fall back into the trap of being a home for terrorist activities. Immediately upon completion of combat operations, water trucks, food & water drops, and other humanitarian assistance missions became the standard throughout Tal Afar.[69]

Over the course of October and November, the Coalition initiated projects worth millions of dollars focused especially on the restoration of water, electricity, schools, and medical services. Sabre Squadron created a civil military operations center in the city that became a focal point for interacting with the local population on a wide variety of issues. Similarly, Sabre Squadron Soldiers were active in rejuvenating the city council and several other municipal institutions.[70]

The Coalition's spending in Tal Afar via the Commander's Emergency Response Program (CERP) also rose dramatically in the fall of 2005. As outlined in the previous chapter, this program provides money that brigade commanders and their subordinate commanders can use to meet local needs in their areas of operation. CERP funds typically go to relatively small, relatively short-term projects, and also pay reparations for property damaged in combat or to family members of killed and wounded civilians. Estimated CERP spending in Tal Afar increased significantly over the period of the case study. Estimated spending by quarter rose from $399,000 (May-July) to $418,000 (August-October) to $1.1 million (November-January) to $1.3 million (February-April).[71] This represents an increase from beginning to end of a factor of 3.3. See Figure 3-3.

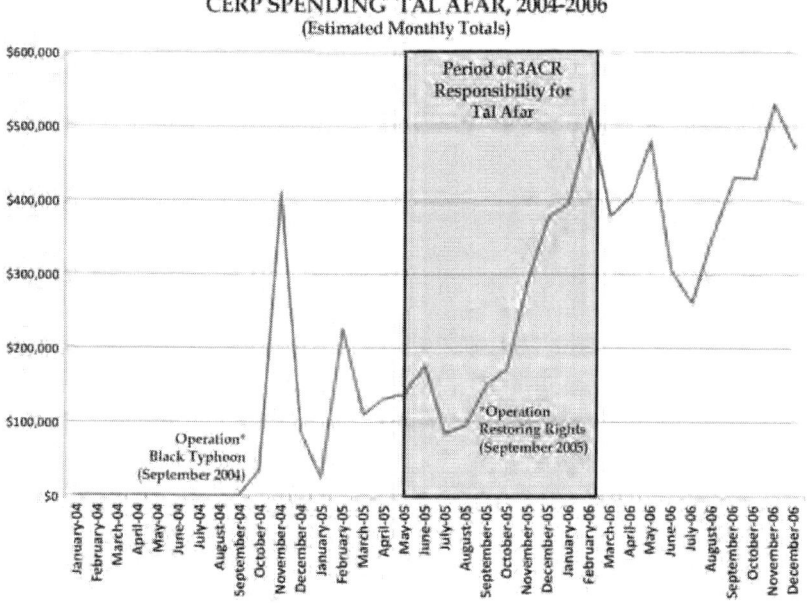

CERP SPENDING TAL AFAR, 2004-2006
(Estimated Monthly Totals)

**Figure 3-3. Estimated Monthly CERP Spending in Tal Afar.**

The results of these large investments, not only CERP, but other investments made by the Coalition and the Iraqi government, were evident in relatively short order. Tal Afar's markets and schools re-opened, and basic services were gradually restored to some level of working order. A British reporter visiting Tal Afar in December 2005 reported that:

the streets are full of building sites. New sewers have been dug and the fronts of shops, destroyed in the U.S. assault, were replaced within weeks. Sunni police have been hired and 2,000 goats were even distributed to farmers. More remarkably, the approach of an American military convoy brings people out to wave and even clap.[72]

Some interviewees noted the importance of improvements in governance in building the legitimacy of the Coalition and the local government in the eyes of the local population. One U.S. squad leader called the difference made "night and day — people really appreciated it."[73] A troop commander said, "The population continuously gave us praise for what we did there. They were very appreciative and looked on us favorably."[74] An engineering platoon leader believed that, "Improving those kinds of quality-of-life conditions was one of the most important things that swayed the population over to supporting the Coalition."[75]

At the same time, as in Ramadi, some interviewees noted serious limitations to the effects of some of the reconstruction projects pursued, and believed that the local population was far more interested in and appreciative of the security provided by the Coalition. A regimental staff officer commented that "We dumped a ton of money into construction projects that they weren't interested in — schools, parks, etc."[76] A reporter who spent a few months in Tal Afar during this period commented that "People would always complain about water and electricity. . . [But] that whole argument about basic services – the main public utility is security. This is more important than anything else."[77] Another interviewee, Lieutenant Tinklepaugh, stated plainly that:

the reconstruction activities that we engaged in were a consequence of our success in marginalizing the insurgency, not a cause of it. The population was appreciative, but they rarely commented on it. What they were much more appreciative of was the security . . . They were real upset about the lack of electricity and the lack of water pressure (and these problems exacerbated each other). And this created a problem with the sewage system, which was also exacerbated by all of the drainage issues created by the problems in the streets – caused by our vehicles as well as by the combat. But these problems didn't cause people to want to become insurgents, it caused people to become apathetic.[78]

3ACR's commander, Colonel McMaster, seemed to share this perspective, arguing that:

The most important thing is securing the population. And you can't do much positive until you've established this. . . . Governance projects were important factors in our progress, but they came at a different time—it was more of a reward for cooperation. It happened in areas that were already secured.[79]

## Were Political Agreements Addressing Ethno-Religious Cleavages Pursued?

From fairly early in 3ACR's deployment, its leaders focused on the importance of reaching a political accommodation among Tal Afar's tribal groups, whose increasingly sectarian loyalties were pushing the city toward something like civil war. Lieutenant Colonel Hickey was the regiment's point person in this effort, and by all accounts he focused tirelessly on building relationships with Tal Afar's sheikhs and on attempting to bridge the divides between them.

Initially, as noted, only the Shi'a sheikhs were willing to talk seriously with U.S. leaders about the future of the city. Hickey began spending 40 or 50 hours a week with the Sunni sheikhs, working to convince them of the U.S. commitment to securing their people. Then just as Hickey began to make inroads with Sunni sheikhs, "the Shia freaked out," as Hickey told journalist George Packer. They questioned the purpose of, as they viewed it, consorting with the enemy. "Because I'm trying to be balanced," Hickey recalled telling the Shi'a leaders. "I'm trying to stabilize your city. If I just talk to you, I'm not going to stabilize your city."[80]

This shift toward cultivating relationships among the Sunnis was not necessarily an intuitive choice on the U.S. side either. "At the troop level," Captain Jesse Sellars said, "this was unpopular, because this means we have to go make friends with the guys who are blowing us up instead of with the guys who are feeding us fried chicken. But [Hickey] was absolutely right."[81]

Whenever possible, Hickey tried to arrange and moderate meetings among sheikhs where they could air grievances with each other and with U.S. forces and discuss potential resolutions. In time, one theme Hickey came to stress in such meetings and that the regiment tried to impress more broadly upon the city's residents, was the common cause Tal Afar's Sunnis and Shi'a ought to share against the terrorism perpetrated against them by the "Takfiris." As Hickey described, "the 'Resistance' had the potential to be quelled through involvement in the ongoing political process *IF* they could escape the intimidation campaign of the [insurgents] living among them."[82] In Major Simmering's view, the real purpose of Operation RESTORING RIGHTS was not "to clear the town of insurgents . . . it was to protect the Sunni population who were willing to participate in the political process."[83]

After Operation RESTORING RIGHTS, rebuilding the police force also became one of 3ACR's most important tools for addressing the sectarian conflicts in the city. Abuses by the Shi'a police force had been a major contributing factor to Tal Afar's downward spiral, and as a result, U.S. forces believed that "the first step toward reconciliation among the populace meant recreating a police force that was representative of the population."[84] Police recruiting focused heavily on the city's Sunni population.

The insurgents may well have recognized the strategic importance of this development and tried to counter it. In the first several weeks after the end of Operation RESTORING RIGHTS, Tal Afar was rocked by three major suicide bombing attacks, which together killed around 70 people and injured more than 130 others.[85] Two of these three attacks were directed specifically at police recruits. Nevertheless, the police recruiting efforts remained a focus of the regiment's strategy, and ultimately saw a great deal of success. By the end of its deployment in Tal Afar, 1,400 new police officers had been recruited, 60 percent of whom were Sunnis.[86]

The rebalancing of the police force was part of a broader attempt by the 3ACR's leadership to rebuild a sense of national identity in the city. As the regiment's executive officer, Major Chris Kennedy, told a reporter, "What we're working toward is a national army, a national security force, not a Shiite or a Kurdish force, and anyone who thinks otherwise doesn't know the situation."[87] George Packer describes seeing Lieutenant Colonel Hickey "ask a group of police trainees at a new station whether they were Sunni or Shiite, and when they started to answer, he said, 'No — Iraqi!'"[88]

In combination with all of the Coalition's other operations, these political overtures aimed at reducing sectarian antagonism did appear to pay off over time as the city's sheikhs began to take steps toward aligning their own activities with those of the nascent city government, as well as with the counterinsurgency goals of the U.S. and Iraqi security forces. A 3 ACR intelligence officer described the progress he saw over the fall of 2005:

> The real difference since ORR has been in the reporting and cooperation from the locals, both Shia and Sunni, to turn in anyone who is causing problems and there have even been fights reported between Sunni groups as the previously-intimated are fighting back, even against members of their own tribe or sect. The long-simmering feud in Tal Afar between the Shia Jolaqs and the Sunni Farhats . . . has cooled down significantly after several weeks of sheikh meetings to iron out their long-running disputes.[89]

In describing the evolution of the meeting with the city's sheikhs, Major Simmering said, "Where we got to wasn't perfect, but what was a screaming match in June was a civil conversation in January."[90]

None of this means to imply that the sectarian conflicts that had created so much strife had been solved. Indeed, the wounds of the tribal feuding ran deep, even though they were young in historical terms. Those tensions and grievances persisted. Sectarian murders continued, and discrimination on the basis of sect and tribal affiliation was rampant. In December, a self-appointed council of sheikhs and clerics published a formal statement complaining about the persecution of the Sunni population in Tal Afar.[91]

Tal Afar's reformed police were not necessarily a picture of professionalism or blind justice. George

Packer had this exchange with an officer named Hassan once during his visit in early 2006. Hassan told Packer:

> If the Americans weren't here, we could get more out of our interrogations.
> You mean torture?
> Only the terrorists.
> How many terrorists and sympathizers are there in Tal Afar?
> Hassan considered it for a moment. "A hundred and fifty thousand." This was approximately the number of Sunnis in the city.[92]

What the record does demonstrate, however, is that the U.S. forces fighting the counterinsurgency in Tal Afar were keenly aware of the sectarian roots of some of the insurgency they were facing and took deliberate and extensive measures to reach accommodation between competing sectarian parties. As journalist Louise Roug observed, "the military leadership had a very sophisticated understanding of the groups in the city, and who was aggrieved and why. They did try to prop up the groups who felt disenfranchised."[93]

### Was The Counterinsurgency Successful?

According to journalist Tom Ricks, "When U.S. military experts conducted an internal review of the three dozen major U.S. brigades, battalions, and similar units operating in Iraq in 2005, they concluded that of all those units, the 3rd ACR had done the best at counterinsurgency."[94] There is no doubt that 3ACR's operations in Tal Afar have been widely perceived by policymakers and the press as a model of successful counterinsurgency. As noted above, the experience was cited in this vein by, among others, the military's counterinsurgency manual, Secretary of State Condoleezza Rice, and President George Bush.

This view was not exclusive to Americans. During Operation RESTORING RIGHTS, Iraqi Defense Minister, Sa'dun al-Dulaymi (a Sunni Arab) told the press that Iraq's leaders "consider what is going on there an example and a model to be followed in other areas . . . in Iraq."[95]

During 3ACR's deployment, Tal Afar mayor Najim Abdullah al-Jabouri asked for the regiment's tour to be extended and wrote a letter of glowing tribute to the unit. He credited the regiment with liberating the city, transforming it "from a ghost town, in which terrorists spread death and destruction, to a secure city flourishing with life." He said, "This military operation was clean, with little collateral damage, despite the ferocity of the enemy. With the skill and precision of surgeons, they dealt with the terrorist cancers in the city without causing unnecessary damage." He called the American Soldiers "not only courageous men and women, but avenging angels sent by The God Himself. . . ."[96] Even allowing for some inevitable public relations spin[97] and Arabic hyperbole, this registers as high praise.

Sabre Squadron summed up its own performance as follows:

> . . . the 1,300 cavalrymen of Sabre Squadron decisively defeated the insurgents, re-established legitimate security forces at nearly 41 locations throughout the area and revived a local government and economy on the brink of annihilation. . . the citizens of Tal Afar and the surrounding areas. . . acknowledge that participation in the political process is the primary avenue to a future peace in Iraq.[98]

107

The regiment listed the following comparisons of the "enemy situation" in its area of operations near the beginning and the end of its deployment.[99] See Table 3-1.

| June 2005 | January 2006 |
|---|---|
| • Enemy retained the initiative, capable of complex attacks and defensive operations<br>• Western Ninewah avenue for insurgents and access to external support<br>• Tal Afar safe haven for leadership and "Title 10" functions<br>• HUMINT access limited<br>• Organization was cohesive and militarily structured<br>• Multiple cells in urban areas<br>• Tribal violence pervasive | • Enemy reactive, only capable of IED and IDF attacks<br>• Western Ninewah difficult to traverse with reduced external support<br>• Tal Afar now a non-permissive environment<br>• HUMINT unlimited<br>• Leadership disrupted and displaced<br>• Few cells operating in small communities outside urban areas<br>• Tribal tensions exist, no open violence |

**Table 3-1. Changes in Western Ninewah, June 2005 – January 2006.**

These assessments are supported by the striking drop in insurgent attacks experienced in this time period and shown in Figure 3-2. Interviewees universally, albeit with varying degrees of qualification, described Tal Afar as a counterinsurgency success story.

As with any celebrated event, a certain mythology has developed around the 3ACR's experience in Tal Afar, and in fact, the success the regiment enjoyed there was not as "decisive" as the paeans above suggest. There were troubling signs just a month after the regiment left Iraq. One resident told a reporter, "the armed men are fewer, but the assassinations between

Sunni and Shiites have increased." Another resident said, "Al-Qaeda has started to come back again. They have started to kill Shiites and Sunnis who cooperate with the Americans."[100] Another report suggested that "Fear is palpable in the streets. . . . Residents complain that the city is increasingly divided as tribal violence sharpens the boundaries between Sunni and and Shiite Muslim neighborhoods." Even with a large Iraqi and U.S. troop presence, "families complain of no-go areas in the city, boundaries drawn up by sectarian violence or intimidation by rebels."[101] The insurgency continued in western Ninewah province, and U.S. forces continued to fight there for months and years after the period of this case study.

Moreover, interviewees fully acknowledged the fragility of the stability that Tal Afar had attained on their watch. In one platoon leader's judgment,

> We defeated the insurgency, but we weren't really able to rebuild the government—there wasn't enough time for that. . . . When I first saw the city on April 21 or so, it was just an absolute ghost town. That day seven IEDs went off, people were shooting, everybody in the city was hiding from us, but watching us. Compare that to the last patrol I did on February 13, the market was open, the place was mobbed, there was garbage pick-up, we were talking to people . . . That said, for the most part, people still tended to stick to their areas. The neighborhoods remained somewhat segregated, like Route Barracuda, everything south was Shi'a, everything north was Sunni, and many people were not comfortable crossing that line.[102]

A regimental staff officer concluded:

> I certainly won't say we solved or defeated the insurgency throughout the province. I will say, though,

that with the help of very effective Iraqi leaders . . . we were able to establish security conditions that allowed progress in security force development and essential services.[103]

Tal Afar never fell back into the terrorized state of dysfunction that it had suffered through during 2004-05. The alliance that had formed between the Sunni tribes and the Islamist extremists of AQI was radically diminished. A reporter visiting Tal Afar in April 2006 was told by a Soldier in the city's operations center that there were then three to five sectarian murders a week in the city. The Coalition did not seem especially concerned about it, and the reporter said, "At that time, this sounded like success to me too, not only compared to other places in the country, but also compared to Tal Afar the previous year."[104]

This is where the difference between "victory" and "success" becomes analytically important. Counterinsurgency operations in Tal Afar during this period did not result in victory in the sense that they ended the insurgency. But it is more than fair to call the 3ACR's achievements there a success on the basis of the significant and lasting gains in security made there.

**Evaluation.**

Table 3-2 summarizes the simple answers for the study's framework questions that are suggested by the evidence presented in this chapter. Conditions for positive answers for all five variables were present in this case. Sunni-Shi'a conflict was very clearly central to the insurgency, not only along the local-national axis as in Ramadi, but also along local tribal axes. On balance, counterinsurgents conducted good security operations. Following Operation RESTORING RIGHTS, the Coalition committed a large number of troops to security, kept them living among the people to focus better on population security, and worked closely with relatively professional indigenous security forces. And the counterinsurgents dedicated significant resources, manpower, and leadership focus both to improving governance in the city and to working toward political agreements among the city's warring groups that would address their sectarian and tribal grievances.

| Cases | Identity Cleavages | Good Security | Good Governance | Political Agreement | Success |
|-------|--------------------|---------------|-----------------|---------------------|---------|
| Tal Afar 2005-2006 | Yes | Yes | Yes | Yes | Yes |

**Table 3-2. Case Study Variable Summary for Tal Afar.**

From an analytic perspective, success in the Tal Afar case was overdetermined, thereby clouding any effort to parse the relative contributions to success of different factors. This is where the opinions of participants on causation must be given special weight.

Even here, though, the evidence is mixed. Some interviewees emphasized the dominant role of the force density that the United States was able to bring to bear in Tal Afar. Tiger Squadron's commander, Lieutenant Colonel Greg Reilly, argued that "saturating the area with forces is guaranteed to have a major effect. Up until the regiment left, it still had a pretty sizable footprint in the city, and this accounts for a lot of the improvement in security and stability. But there was still a high level of sectarian tension."[105]

Other 3ACR Soldiers certainly saw some causal connection between their initiatives to improve governance and the marginalization of the insurgents in Tal Afar. Sabre Squadron troop commander Captain Sellars laid out the case for this logic succinctly: "Getting people back to a more normal life, giving them something to lose, provides the foundation for getting more to the political processes, and addressing tribal and sectarian differences."[106] Lieutenant Colonel Chris Gibson, who commanded 2-325 in the Sarai neighborhood, later wrote, "The nascent governing entity must provide basic services to bolster its legitimacy with the people. . . . The water and electricity departments were key — they must be effective and impartial in the distribution of service."[107] Lieutenant Colonel Hickey, in many ways the principal architect of the Tal Afar success, concluded that "the ability of the Squadron to enable the Iraqi Government to meet the needs of the population served to strengthen relations between the local government and the populace as well as establish a path toward reconciliation."[108] Here the implied causal chain goes from government performance to political reconciliation among competing groups.

But in the very same document, in explaining the strategic logic behind Operation RESTORING RIGHTS, Hickey also says:

> . . . by [the Coalition] attacking the Takfirists and guarding against the tendency to attack the population directly, the Sunni could be reintegrated into the mainstream political process once the veil of terror was lifted from their ranks. Meanwhile, maintaining the support of the Shiites could eventually bring unity to the city and establish an environment that finally allowed for reconstruction operations and reconciliation of tribal conflicts.[109]

In this description, the apparent causal chain runs from political reconciliation to improved government performance, not the other way around. This logic matches two of the comments cited earlier in the chapter: Lieutenant Tinklepaugh's assertion that "the reconstruction activities that we engaged in were a consequence of our success in marginalizing the insurgency, not a cause of it"[110]; and Colonel McMaster's observation that "Governance projects were important factors in our progress, but they came at a different time — it was more of a reward for cooperation. It happened in areas that were already secured."[111]

Of course, some indeterminate degree of security must precede both of those other factors. Lieutenant Colonel Gibson, while lauding the importance of "basic services," also argues that "No amount of money or kindness, and no number of infrastructure programs, will facilitate winning over the populace if COIN forces cannot provide security to the population."[112]

Are these counterinsurgents contradicting each other and themselves? That is one plausible interpretation of the evidence. Equally plausible, however, is that these perspectives on causal relationships are compatible with each other. By this logic, because the variables are at least somewhat mutually dependent, different causal directions among the variables may predominate at different times. The implication of this explanation would be that it may not be possible to draw a more precise conclusion than that a positive value for each of the variables may be necessary but not sufficient by itself for success in counterinsurgency. In his own summation of what accounted for his squadron's success, Hickey takes just this approach and does not discriminate among factors:

The cumulative effect of Sunni participation in the political process, establishment of security throughout the city, reconstruction, money distribution, positioning of [2-325] in Sarai, and the establishment of a comprehensive reconnaissance and surveillance plan resulted in a dramatic drop in attacks during the period following [Operation RESTORING RIGHTS].[113]

McMaster seemed to be of a similar mind, observing near the end of 3ACR's tour, "It is so damn complex. If you ever think you have the solution to this, you're wrong, and you're dangerous."[114]

## ENDNOTES - CHAPTER 3

1. Richard A. Oppel, Jr., "Magnet For Iraq Insurgents Is A Crucial Test Of New U.S. Strategy," *New York Times*, June 16, 2005, p. 1.

2. *Baseline Food Security Analysis in Iraq*, p. 105.

3. Interview 12 (First Lieutenant Brian Tinklepaugh); Interview 17 (First Lieutenant Gavin Schwan); Interview 30 (Lieutenant Colonel Greg Reilly).

4. Zeynep Gurcanli, "Why Tall Afar?" *Istanbul Star*, September 17, 2004, FBIS Report GMP20040917000111; Hashim, p. 370.

5. 3rd Armored Cavalry Regiment, "Operation Restoring Rights O&I Update," unpublished briefing, August 27, 2005.

6. Hashim, p. 373.

7. Interview 14 (Colonel H. R. McMaster); Interview 17 (First Lieutenant Gavin Schwan); "Interview with Lieutenant Colonel Paul Yingling," from the collection *Operational Leadership Experiences in the Global War on Terrorism*, Ft. Leavenworth, KS: Combat Studies Institute, September 22, 2006, p. 5.

8. Interview 12 (First Lieutenant Brian Tinklepaugh).

9. Steve Fainaru, "U.S.-Led Forces Retake Northern Iraqi City," *Washington Post*, September 13, 2004, p. 17.

10. Patrick J. McDonnell, "U.S. Targets 3 Iraqi Cities," *Los Angeles Times*, September 10, 2004, p. 1.

11. Fainaru, "U.S.-Led Forces Retake Northern Iraqi City."

12. *Ibid.*

13. "Turks Angry at U.S. Over Killings in Iraq," *New York Daily News*, September 14, 2004.

14. Lieutenant Colonel Christopher M. Hickey, "Memorandum for Record, 2/3 ACR Actions During Operation Iraqi Freedom (OIF) 04-06," January 30, 2006, p. 5.

15. "3rd ACR Chief: Rebels 'Worst of the Worst,'" *Colorado Springs Gazette*, September 14, 2005.

16. Hashim, p. 379; Borzou Daragahi, "Nationalism Drives Many Insurgents As They Fight U.S.," *San Francisco Chronicle*, October 26, 2004, p. 9; Captain Travis Patriquin, "Using Occam's Razor to Connect the Dots: The Ba'ath Party and the Insurgency in Tal Afar," *Military Review*, January-February 2007, p. 21.

17. Interview 12 (First Lieutenant Brian Tinklepaugh).

18. Interview 10 (Major Michael Simmering).

19. Ricardo A. Herrera, "Brave Rifles at Tall Afar, September 2005," in William G. Robertson, ed., *In Contact! Case Studies from the Long War, Volume I*, Ft. Leavenworth, KS: Combat Studies Institute Press, 2006, pp. 125-152.

20. Interview 17 (First Lieutenant Gavin Schwan).

21. Interview 16 (Second Lieutenant Andrew Shealy).

22. Interview 28 (Captain Alan Blackburn).

23. Interview 12 (First Lieutenant Brian Tinklepaugh).

24. Interview 25 (Colonel Joel Armstrong).

25. Interview 9 (Captain James Dayhoff); Interview 14 (Colonel H. R. McMaster).

26. Oppel.

27. Hickey, p. 12.

28. Oppel.

29. Hickey, p. 30.

30. Interview 12 (First Lieutenant Brian Tinklepaugh).

31. Hickey, pp. 24-25.

32. *Ibid.*, p. 32.

33. Interview 12 (First Lieutenant Brian Tinklepaugh); Interview 30 (Lieutenant Colonel Greg Reilly); Herrera, p. 142.

34. President George W. Bush, Remarks to the City Club of Cleveland, Ohio, March 20, 2006.

35. Hickey, p. 40.

36. *Ibid.*, p. 41.

37. *Ibid.*, pp. 44, 51.

38. *Ibid.*

39. *Ibid.*, p. 51.

40. Peter Baker, "An Iraq Success Story's Sad New Chapter," *Washington Post*, March 21, 2006, p. 1; Louise Roug, "Fear Casts A Shadow On 'Free City' Touted By Bush," *Los Angeles Times*, March 26, 2006.

41. Secretary of State Condoleezza Rice, "Iraq and U.S. Policy," Testimony before the U.S. Senate Committee on Foreign Relations, October 19, 2005.

42. Bush.

43. *Field Manual (FM) 3-24/Marine Corps Warfighting Publication 3-33.5, Counterinsurgency* (FM 3-24/MCWP 3-33.5), pp. 5-22 – 5-23.

44. Hashim, pp. 371-372; Patriquin, p. 17.

45. Hashim, p. 374.

46. Interview 30 ((Lieutenant Colonel Greg Reilly).

47. Interview 24 (anonymous regional specialist).

48. Interview 2 (Louise Roug); Interview 10 (Major Michael Simmering); Interview 11 (Monte Morin); Interview 28 (Captain Alan Blackburn).

49. Interview 21 (Captain Jesse Sellars).

50. Hashim, pp. 374-375, Hickey, p. 3.

51. Jonathan Finer, "Iraqi Forces Show Signs Of Progress In Offensive," *Washington Post*, September 22, 2005, p. 1.

52. Hickey, p. 3.

53. Jonathan Finer, "With Death At Their Door, Few Leave Iraqi City," *Washington Post*, September 7, 2005, p. 20, Interview 2 (Louise Roug).

54. "Defense Minister Discusses Tall Afar, Urges Iraqis To 'Drive Out Terrorists'," *Al-Arabiyah Television*, September 12, 2005, FBIS Report GMP200509125380002.

55. "The Iraqi Scene," *Al-Jazirah Satellite Channel Television*, September 18, 2005, FBIS Report GMP20050918564001.

56. Interview 12 (First Lieutenant Brian Tinklepaugh); Interview 30 (Lieutenant Colonel Greg Reilly).

57. Interview 10 (Major Michael Simmering).

58. Interview 21 (Captain Jesse Sellars).

59. Interview 28 (Captain Alan Blackburn).

60. *Ibid.*, Interview 21 (Captain Jesse Sellars).

61. Hickey, p. 41.

62. Interview 8 (Second Lieutenant Dan Driscoll); Interview 9 (Captain James Dayhoff); Interview 18 (Sergeant Chad Stapp), "Interview with Lieutenant Colonel Paul Yingling," p. 6.

63. Interview 14 (Colonel H. R. McMaster).

64. Interview 17 (First Lieutenant Gavin Schwan); Interview 25 (Colonel Joel Armstrong); Interview 28 (Captain Alan Blackburn); Interview 30 (Lieutenant Colonel Greg Reilly); Herrera, pp. 140-141.

65. Interview 9 (Captain James Dayhoff).

66. Interview 14 (Colonel H. R. McMaster).

67. Oppel.

68. First Lieutenant Brian Tinklepaugh, personal correspondence with the author, April 10, 2009.

69. Hickey, p. 39.

70. *Ibid.*, p. 42.

71. Iraqi Reconstruction Management System, U. S. Army Corps of Engineers, Gulf Region Division, June 2008. Available data on Commander's Emergency Response Program (CERP) spending totals include total funds distributed and project start dates and end dates. The author has estimated monthly

and quarterly spending totals based on equal division of total funds spent over the number of active months per project. Project lengths in the database range from 1 to 40 months, but the average length is 4 months. As a result, aggregate quarterly spending summaries (as reported in the text above) are less likely to be distorted by this estimation technique than the monthly spending estimates (as shown in the figure).

72. Oliver Poole, "Iraqis In Former Rebel Stronghold Now Cheer American Soldiers," *The Daily Telegraph*, December 19, 2005.

73. Interview 18 (Sergeant Chad Stapp).

74. Interview 28 (Captain Alan Blackburn).

75. Interview 20 (Second Lieutenant Jared Leinart).

76. Interview 9 (Captain James Dayhoff).

77. Interview 11 (Monte Morin).

78. Interview 12 (First Lieutenant Brian Tinklepaugh).

79. Interview 14 (Colonel H. R. McMaster).

80. Packer, p. 53.

81. Interview 21 (Captain Jesse Sellars).

82. Hickey, p. 23 (emphasis in original).

83. Interview 10 (Major Michael Simmering).

84. Hickey, p. 41.

85. Sabrina Tavernise, "Suicide Blast by Woman in Iraq Kills 8 Others; 57 Are Hurt," *New York Times*, September 29, 2005; Associated Press, "More Than 50 Dead Following Series of Attacks," *USA Today*, October 12, 2005, p. 13; Louise Roug, "Suicide Attack Kills 30 in Northern Iraq," *Los Angeles Times*, October 13, 2005.

86. Thomas E. Ricks, "The Lessons of Counterinsurgency," *Washington Post*, February 16, 2006, p. 14.

87. Finer, "Iraqi Forces Show Signs of Progress In Offensive."

88. Packer, p. 54.

89. Craig T. Olson, *So This Is War: A 3rd U.S. Cavalry Intelligence Officer's Memoirs of the Triumphs, Sorrows, Laughter, and Tears During a Year in Iraq*, Bloomington, IN: AuthorHouse, 2007, p. 132.

90. Interview 10 (Major Michael Simmering).

91. Ferry Biedermann, "Tel Afar's Ethnic Tug of War Puts Iraq Army to the Test," *Financial Times*, January 18, 2006.

92. Packer, p. 56.

93. Interview 2 (Louise Roug).

94. Ricks, *Fiasco: The American Military Adventure in Iraq*, p. 420.

95. "Iraqi Defense Minister Says 18 Arms Caches Found in Tall Afar, Gives Update," *Al-Sharqiyah Television*, September 11, 2005, FBIS Report, GMP20050911538001.

96. Quoted in Olson, pp. 193-194. The letter recalls a similar letter sent from an Algerian town mayor to French Army Captain David Galula where the future counterinsurgency theorist had led French efforts to improve both security and governance. See David Galula, *Pacification in Algeria (1956-1958)*, Santa Monica, CA: RAND Corporation, 1963, p. 232.

97. As one interviewee pointed out, Mayor Najim was not from Tal Afar and may have owed his position to the Coalition. Interview 22 (Jon Finer).

98. Hickey, pp. 1-2.

99. 3rd Armored Cavalry Regiment, "Operations and Intelligence Brief," undated briefing, p. 5. ("Title 10"=training and

equipping, HUMINT=human intelligence, IED=Improvised Explosive Device, IDF=Indirect Fire.)

100.  Baker.

101.  Roug, "Fear Casts A Shadow On 'Free City' Touted By Bush."

102.  Interview 17 (First Lieutenant Gavin Schwan).

103.  "Interview with Lieutenant Colonel Paul Yingling," p. 6.

104.  Interview 11 (Monte Morin).

105.  Interview 30 (Lieutenant Colonel Greg Reilly).

106.  Interview 21 (Captain Jesse Sellars).

107. Lieutenant Colonel Chris Gibson, "Battlefield Victories and Strategic Success: The Path Forward in Iraq," *Military Review*, September-October 2006, p. 54.

108.  Hickey, p. 42.

109. *Ibid.*, p. 32.

110. Interview 12 (First Lieutenant Brian Tinklepaugh).

111. Interview 14 (Colonel H. R. McMaster).

112. Gibson, p. 49.

113. Hickey, p. 46.

114. Packer, p. 57.

# CHAPTER 4

## CONCLUSIONS AND IMPLICATIONS

This final chapter sums up the preceding analysis in four sections: a comparison of the case studies, conclusions, policy implications, and an overview of potential priorities for further research.

## COMPARISON OF THE CASES

Table 4-1 summarizes the answers to each of the analytic framework's questions for the two case studies. The table also includes answers for the Awakening movement in Ramadi and elsewhere in Anbar province during 2006 and 2007. Clearly, as this case was not addressed formally in the analysis, these answers are tentative. But they are included as potentially useful discussion points.

| Cases | Identity Cleavages | Good Security | Good Governance | Political Agreement | Success |
|---|---|---|---|---|---|
| Ramadi 2004-2005 | Yes | Ambiguous | No | No | No |
| Tal Afar | Yes | Yes | Yes | Yes | Yes |
| Ramadi Awakening (notional) | Yes | Ambiguous | Ambiguous | Yes | Yes |

**Table 4-1. Summary for Iraq Case Studies.**

Given these answers, what do the cases say about the primary question of the study: *In the presence of major ethno-religious cleavages, does good governance contribute much less to counterinsurgent success than efforts*

123

*toward reaching political agreements that directly address those cleavages?*

In Ramadi, the grievances that fueled the insurgency had far more to do with a deep sense of disenfranchisement within Iraq's Sunni community and the related fear of sectarian persecution than it did with any failure in the government's performance. The causal links between variations in the quality of governance and the fortunes of the counterinsurgents are difficult to establish precisely given the simultaneous weaknesses of the security and political lines of operation in Ramadi. Nevertheless, the evidence from the interviews in this case points toward major limitations to how much popular loyalty and legitimacy could be won through the improvement of governance. Other factors—namely security, itself, and identity-based concepts of legitimate rule (both tribal and sectarian)—appeared more decisive. This interpretation is strongly supported by the dramatic shift that eventually occurred in Ramadi, which seems to have roots in two key changes: the exhaustion of the population with violence and terror; and a new willingness of the Coalition to decouple the legitimacy of local rule from the legitimacy of national rule.

Tal Afar's story is quite different, but suggests a similar conclusion. There is no doubt that the quality of governance mattered in the way both the population and the counterinsurgents conceived of legitimacy. At the same time, however, it appears that what improvements in governance occurred in Tal Afar were at least as much a consequence as a cause of successful counterinsurgency. Without both the 3ACR's dense presence in the city and its intensive focus on brokering compromises among the city's largely sectarian tribal conflicts, improvements in governance likely would never have taken root. Even recognizing some degree of mutual reinforcement, the dependency of the factors probably did not run in the opposite direction.

Further evidence in support of the general form of the hypothesis can be found in one of the few quantitative analyses of the Iraq war published to date that uses official Department of Defense time-series, district-level data.[1] Authors Eli Berman, Jacob N. Shapiro, and Joseph H. Felter use multivariate econometric techniques to assess the relative importance of, among other things, economic factors and provision of basic services in affecting levels of violence across 104 districts (the sub-provincial administrative level) in Iraq. At first glance, the results of their analysis, which show a correlation between at least the economic dimensions of good governance and subsequent improvements in violence, appear at odds with this monograph's general argument.

However, their conclusions are qualified by two critical factors that actually bring them closer into alignment with the arguments presented here. First, the authors make the following explicit assumption in their model:

> [N]oncombatants decide [about sharing information] on the basis of a rational calculation of self-interest rather than an overwhelming ideological commitment to one side or another. This is not to say that ideological commitment is irrational or unusual, just that on the margin governments can influence noncombatants' decisions by providing services.[2]

This assumption is plausible, but it bypasses the central question at issue regarding the sources of legitimacy. It is difficult to rebut the idea that the mechanisms of loyalty would work as assumed, "on the margin;" but for those marginal effects to be representative of the main dynamics of the system, the noncombatants would need to be basically indifferent between rule by the insurgents and rule by the government apart from the factors of service or retaliation. This premise is not consistent with observed group solidarity of various kinds, including ethno-religious.

The other critical caveat to this analysis is that it shows that up until 2007, Commander's Emergency Response Program (CERP) spending, the model's proxy for service provision, had essentially no effect in reducing violence. Only beginning in 2007 — a very different environment from previous years due to the Awakening and the Coalition troop "surge" — does the beneficial effect of CERP spending become evident.[3] The authors attribute this change to the military's improved ability to garner intelligence in part because of its better integration with the population, but mainly because tribes were willing to share information. This explanation is fine as far as it goes, but what accounts for the shift, itself?

The Ramadi case here suggests that the shift had much to do with a change in the Coalition's political strategy as it related to Iraq's sectarian rivalries. Specifically, in 2004-05, U.S. policy was to insist that Coalition cooperation with the Sunni tribal groups in Anbar was contingent on their integration into the security mechanisms of the federal government. This was a deal breaker for the tribes because they viewed the federal government as a tool of Shi'a sectarian interests. Those political institutions were illegitimate by virtue of their perceived identity. Cooperation became possible only when the Coalition decoupled its own support from the requirement to integrate with Baghdad. By this logic, it was not primarily better intelligence that allowed CERP to have its natural salutary effect. Instead, what made the difference was the establishment of an authority, in the form of tribal leaders, who had both capacity and local legitimacy, both of which had been lacking theretofore. So the service provision improvements followed the legitimacy, not the other way around.

## CONCLUSIONS

1. Identity politics shape counterinsurgency outcomes. The case studies presented here demonstrate the importance of ethno-religious identity politics in shaping the outcomes of insurgencies and counterinsurgencies. In both cases, direct causal relationships are evident between the counterinsurgents' attentiveness to the politics of ethno-religious identity and the subsequent course of the insurgencies.

In Ramadi and Tal Afar, competition between insurgents and counterinsurgents over the quality of governance was a clearly less important factor in determining the conflict outcomes than the disposition of political agreements related to ethno-religious cleavages. Furthermore, though the evidence is not conclusive, it is even plausible that providing good governance was neither necessary nor sufficient for achieving counterinsurgent success.

This is not to say, however, that providing good governance was irrelevant. Even if good governance is evidently less important than cross-cleavage political agreements, it still is shown in the case studies to be a contributor to counterinsurgent success, and its absence an impediment to success. The policy implication of this conclusion about the relative importance of providing good governance is not that counterinsurgents should ignore the quality of governance in the places they are fighting. Rather, it is that they should not invest all their hope of establishing legitimacy through activities focused on improving governance.

2. Identity politics are local. One implication of the first conclusion is the need for a subtle shift in analytic and planning emphasis away from considering individual loyalties and preferences toward considering group loyalties and preferences. However, this shift in emphasis should not be extended to its logical extreme, which would be an assumption that ethno-religious groups will be reliably similar across wide swaths of geography, time, and circumstance. That assumption is not valid. Iraq demonstrates that national-level observations of identity-group politics in the midst of counterinsurgency are relevant but inadequate guides to explaining and affecting local behavior.

Tal Afar's sectarian conflict certainly mirrored Iraq's national sectarian conflict in some ways. But both the conflict's escalation and its subsequent moderation in 2005-06 were driven primarily by local grievances, local conditions, and local compromises. The connection between Tal Afar's Sunni-Shi'a political rivalries and those in Baghdad were much more symbolic than causal. Even in Ramadi, where sectarian conflict existed primarily in relation to Baghdad, not locally, the fortunes of the counterinsurgents turned at least as much on local manifestations of those identity politics as on national ones. Specifically, the tribal Awakening movement that did so much to undermine the insurgency in Anbar province did not result from the successful resolution of national issues that were dividing Sunni and Shi'a, such as constitutional provisions for power sharing, federalism, allocation of oil revenues, or control of federal ministries. To the contrary, the Awakening occurred in spite of ongoing rancor over these issues in Baghdad. Instead, the transformation in Anbar was based, in combination with mounting popular frustration with al-Qaeda, on the Coalition's willingness to expand tribal and other local leaders' degree of control over their own territory and people.

It seems clear that local legitimacy and loyalty develop with a significant degree of independence from national identity group dynamics and institutions. A cavalry troop commander summed it up this way:

> Ninety percent of the population does not look at the situation from a strategic standpoint. They think of it as 'how does this affect me on my block.' They're not just neutral, waiting to be influenced — they're leaning. But they will be strongly influenced by what happens on their own blocks.[4]

3. Population security is still the most important factor in shaping counterinsurgency outcomes. Recognizing the importance of ethno-religious identity politics should do nothing to take away from the fundamental primacy of population security in counterinsurgency strategy. This conclusion is not new, but the case studies clearly underscore the point, so it bears repeating here. Almost all of the counterinsurgents interviewed for this research emphasized the criticality of establishing people's confidence in their own physical security as a prerequisite for accomplishing anything else in a counterinsurgency environment. Civilian analyst Andrea Jackson, who conducted hundreds of interviews with Iraqis during 2003-06, reported that "I asked every person I interviewed . . . what's the biggest concern for you and your family? They all said security, uniformly."[5]

These conclusions do not overturn any of the traditional tenets of counterinsurgency, but instead should help to sharpen some of them. Based on this research the conventional wisdom that successful counterinsurgency depends on establishing legitimacy, which in turn demands coordinated political and military programs, remains valid. To the extent that "winning hearts and minds" describes this principle, that phrase remains applicable.

What this research adds to our understanding of counterinsurgency is an appreciation for identity-based sources of legitimacy which can rival and even eclipse the legitimacy that flows from good governance. Accordingly, the political component of a counterinsurgency strategy must be political not only in the sense of being focused on government and how government exercises power. It must also be sensitive to the distribution of that power across key identity groups.

## POLICY IMPLICATIONS

Moving from description and analytic inference to prescription is an inevitably treacherous step on the scholarly path. Few single studies of complex social phenomena can hope to be comprehensive or definitive enough to produce unambiguous policy recommendations with much confidence.

On the other hand, the applicability of the work's insights to real world problems is, in the end, one of the most important measures of its quality. While this study's results are far from the final word on its subject, they do suggest several important implications for policymakers and counterinsurgent leaders.

1. Counterinsurgency strategy must account for the role of traditional social hierarchies and forms of legitimacy. The intermediation of relationships between people and their government by tribes or clerics or other nongovernmental group leaders is a strategically important factor in counterinsurgency. Iraq is a clear illustration that these traditional hierarchies can be relevant even in societies that appear in many respects to be quite modern or developed according to the Western model. This creates an imperative for counterinsurgents, at a minimum, to understand what power hierarchies exist among the people where they are fighting, and to explicitly examine the role of group loyalty and identity politics in their assessments of their operational environment. In instances where these factors appear salient, they must become integral to strategy development as well. These traditional hierarchies and identity-based loyalties may be potential assets for the counterinsurgents, or they may be obstacles to their larger strategic goals.

Or, as with the tribes of Anbar province, they may be assets and obstacles simultaneously. Empowering those tribes was a step backward in the Coalition's effort to create a strong, unified central government, but at the same time was critically important in undermining the worst elements of the insurgency. Even participants in the counterinsurgency during that time may continue to differ about whether the proper trade-off was made in that case.[6] All the same, it is not necessary to settle this point in order to simply recognize the utility of anticipating the importance of such trade-offs in advance rather than stumbling upon them a few months or years into a conflict. That is what makes this factor a critical element of the initial assessment and strategy development phase for any prospective counterinsurgency.

2. Counterinsurgents should always prepare to employ the full range of tools addressing security, governance and identity. David Galula believed that each military, political, judicial, and other line of operation in counterinsurgency is indispensible, arguing that "if one is nil, the product will be zero."[7] This may not always be the case, but it remains a valid, conservative guide to planning.

Notwithstanding the emphasis on the potentially high importance of addressing ethno-religious cleavages, the dynamics of identity politics and group loyalties are likely to be so fluid, opaque, and variable across localities that counterinsurgents cannot afford to neglect any element of its legitimacy-building tool kit. They should prepare to build political stability on foundations of both identity and quality of governance simultaneously. This is not to say that it is impossible to make distinctions about where certain tools may be more or less effective. Rather, it is saying that the complexity and uncertainty associated with the problem recommends a conservative approach that does not exclude any potentially valuable contributor to building support of the people for the counterinsurgent's control.

To reiterate the point made under the first conclusion above, the policy implication of recognizing the limitations of providing good governance is not that counterinsurgents should ignore the quality of governance in the places they are fighting. Rather, it is just that counterinsurgents should adopt a heightened sense of caution regarding what can be achieved through improving governance alone in the absence of the larger political strategy that addresses power distributions among identity groups.

3. Local, specialized knowledge trumps doctrine and theory. Because the dynamics of insurgency and

counterinsurgency are so sensitive to variations in local conditions and events, strategies should be based to the maximum extent possible on local, specialized knowledge and relationships. Counterinsurgency doctrine and theory are useful for providing frameworks and guidelines for strategy development, but in developing strategies for particular conflicts, as David Kilcullen said:

> There is simply no substitute for what we might call 'conflict ethnography': a deep, situation-specific understanding of the human, social, and cultural dimensions of a conflict, understood not by analogy with some other conflict, but in its own terms.[8]

4. Do not economize on force size. No matter how sophisticated the counterinsurgency strategy, it is unlikely to succeed without the allocation of enough security forces to create a visible and ubiquitous presence where the insurgency is active. Case study interviewees consistently reported that some degree of physical population security was a pre-requisite for gaining traction on any other element of the counterinsurgency strategy. The contrast between the two case studies illustrates the value of large densities of troops in urban counterinsurgency as well as the challenges of spreading troops thinly. Stalin's famous dictum on conventional war applies to irregular warfare just as well: quantity has a quality all its own.

5. Avoid getting involved in counterinsurgency. One final implication of this research is simply a reinforcement of the enduring and yet apparently unpersuasive point that winning counterinsurgencies is extremely difficult, especially for foreign powers. In important respects, the issues at stake in insurgencies are not especially amenable to change through

the instruments of foreign governments and militaries. For governments under attack, of course, this is a moot point. However, for governments making commitments beyond their borders to fight this kind of warfare, it is quite salient. While the track record of counterinsurgency is not entirely one of failure, it is universally one of costs and complications that far exceeded initial expectations.

## PRIORITIES FOR FURTHER RESEARCH

An almost unavoidable hazard of research is raising as many or more questions as one has answered. This research is no exception. Additionally, there are many ways in which the analysis could be strengthened. Some of the most potentially valuable priorities for further research on this subject are as follows.

A key limitation of the analysis presented here is the absence of significant input from Iraqi sources. Practical considerations prevented collection of much of this kind of data, but clearly, a fuller examination of how Iraqis think about legitimacy and the politics of ethno-religious identity would include the results of direct discussions with Iraqis, themselves. If this research inspires further work on Iraq or any other cases of counterinsurgency or civil conflict, investigators should certainly seek opportunities where possible to draw in perspectives of the people whose loyalty and security is being contested.

Future research on this topic may also benefit from employing an analytic framework somewhat more complex than the one used in this study. Complex frameworks have clear drawbacks, and the relative simplicity of the five-variable framework employed here was adopted purposefully, in part so as to capture the kinds of intuitive categories of decision variables that actually prevail in real policymaking. However, there is a price to pay for this strategy in terms of precise specification and explicit inclusion of some variables. Accordingly, the analytic strategy adopted herein would be well-complemented by research using a more detailed framework with a larger number of more specific variables.

This analysis would also certainly benefit from inclusion of a larger number of case studies. Small numbers of case studies inevitably constrain the process of generalizing insights to draw conclusions and derive recommendations for policy and strategy.

Finally, though further analysis of these topics would not be limited to recent American experiences with counterinsurgency, it is worth noting that more detailed analysis of more local cases should become increasingly feasible as data from Coalition operations in Iraq and Afghanistan becomes more available, in both classified and unclassified contexts. Those experiences will provide a rich basis for comparative case analysis of counterinsurgency for the next generation of scholars and analysts and beyond.

## CONCLUDING THOUGHTS

A U.S. Army veteran of both Iraq and Afghanistan wrote that "The problem with war narratives isn't lying. The problem is there's too much truth. . . . The enterprise is so vast that almost everything is true, and writers can choose whichever truths support a particular thesis."[9] Even as an analyst armed with data and the time to think long and hard about the problem, it is difficult to avoid drawing the same conclusion as this veteran does. Few hypotheses about insurgency and counterinsurgency seem to be completely without evidence, and even fewer seem immune to counterexamples.

But if this research has done nothing else, it has highlighted one truth about counterinsurgency to place alongside the others: that who governs can be even more important than how they govern.

## ENDNOTES - CHAPTER 4

1. Eli Berman, Jacob N. Shapiro, and Joseph H Felter, "Can Hearts and Minds Be Bought? The Economics of Counterinsurgency in Iraq," *Journal of Political Economy*, Vol. 119, No. 4, August 2011.

2. *Ibid.*, p. 776.

3. *Ibid.*, p. 801.

4. Interview 21 (Captain Jesse Sellars).

5. Interview 1 (Andrea Jackson).

6. For example, contrast David Kilcullen, "Anatomy of a Tribal Revolt," *Small Wars Journal Blog*, August 29, 2007; with Austin Long, "The Anbar Awakening," *Survival*, Vol. 50, No. 2, April-May 2008. Both Kilcullen and Long were advisors to Coalition forces during that time.

7. David Galula, *Counterinsurgency Warfare: Theory and Practice,* New York: Frederick A. Praeger, 1964, p. 87.

8. David Kilcullen, "Religion and Insurgency," *Small Wars Journal Blog*, May 12, 2007.

9. Roman Skaskiw, "E-Mail From Afghanistan," *The Atlantic*, October 2008.

Printed in Great Britain
by Amazon.co.uk, Ltd.,
Marston Gate.